Carol Keyes, Director of the Hofstra Child Care Center and mother of three children, trains teachers and is an early childhood curriculum specialist and consultant. She holds a Ph.D. in child development from Union Graduate School in Yellow Springs, Ohio.

Bruce Grossman, a professor at Hofstra University and father of two children, is a clinical psychologist and has done much research and writing on young children. He received his Ph.D. in child development from Duke University in North Carolina.

Together they have written three books.

YOUR CHILDREN, YOUR CHOICES

A Parenting Guide for the Early Years

CAROL KEYES
BRUCE GROSSMAN

A SPECTRUM BOOK

Prentice-Hall, Inc., Englewood Cliffs, N.J. 07632

Library of Congress Cataloging in Publication Data

Keyes, Carol.
     Your children, your choices.

     "A Spectrum Book."
     Includes bibliographies and index.
     1. Parenting—United States.   2. Child rearing—United
States.   I. Grossman, Bruce.   II. Title.
HQ755.8.K49   649'.1   81-15897
                                        AACR2

ISBN 0-13-978221-4

ISBN 0-13-978213-3 {PBK.}

Editorial/production supervision
by Louise M. Marcewicz
Cover design by Jeannette Jacobs
Cover illustration by April Stuart
Manufacturing buyer: Cathie Lenard

This Spectrum Book is available to businesses and organizations
at a special discount when ordered in large quantities. For more
information, contact Prentice-Hall, Inc., General Publishing Division,
Special Sales, Englewood Cliffs, N. J. 07632

Prentice-Hall International, Inc., *London*
Prentice-Hall of Australia Pty. Limited, *Sydney*
Prentice-Hall of Canada, Ltd., *Toronto*
Prentice-Hall of India Private Limited, *New Delhi*
Prentice-Hall of Japan, Inc., *Tokyo*
Prentice-Hall of Southeast Asia Pte. Ltd., *Singapore*
Whitehall Books Limited, *Wellington, New Zealand*

CONTENTS

PREFACE

We have titled this book *Your Children, Your Choices* to under-score the fact that we regard parenting as a serious enterprise that requires more than good intentions. It requires information, thought, and planning. It also requires an open mind. Parenting is a learning experience. It has been our observation that the most effective parenting occurs when parents are able to truly share life experiences with their children and to grow themselves in the process.

Although it is not always easy, parenting can be a major source of pleasure and satisfaction, as many parents will testify. But most parents are, by their own admission, not prepared for the task. As we pointed out in our earlier book:

> Young couples today are more likely to be raising young children apart from their own families in a "nuclear" family situation. Many young parents do not wish to imitate the child-rearing practices of their own parents, and the world for which we are preparing children has become increasingly complex and uncertain.*

In our work with parents, certain concerns resulting from the conditions mentioned above have become apparent to us. These

*Bruce Grossman and Carol Keyes, *Helping Children Grow: The Adult's Role* (Wayne, New Jersey: Avery Publishing Group, 1978), p. vii.

parental concerns are (1) to be better informed about the developmental needs of children; (2) to learn constructive techniques for problem solving and managing the home environment; and (3) to become more aware of their own needs and feelings as they interact with their children. In this book we attempt to address these parental concerns as we encourage parents to grow along with their children.

The book, however, is not specifically devoted to offering child-rearing advice, although we do provide some examples and concrete suggestions. Our primary intention is to share with you, as a parent or a prospective parent, principles of child rearing and information about child development which we have used to create guidelines for raising young children. This should enable you to sort out advice from other sources and to construct a framework for making your own decisions about how you want to raise your child. By integrating our suggestions with your own values and philosophy, you will be able to create your own personal style of relating to your child, a style which is more natural and more useful than any "recipe" that might be handed to you.

In our previous book we focused our efforts on offering ideas to teachers and to other adults working with children in a classroom situation. In this book we are speaking directly to parents and to prospective parents. This is not only a logical extension of our work but an especially important one as well, since parents are the primary adults in a child's life.*

The suggestions and approach in our book for adults working in child care centers apply equally well to parents working with children in their own homes. In fact, many of the parents who have seen our previous book have used some of the ideas successfully in their own homes, and they asked us to translate those principles and suggestions to fit more easily into the home situation.

We have enjoyed the task and hope that you will enjoy the result.

*We wish to be nonsexist in our references to the gender of the "child" being discussed here. In order to deal with the problem, we have decided to alternate the pronoun used in each chapter; that is, we will refer to a child of undisclosed gender as "she" in one chapter and as "he" in the next.

chapter one
INTRODUCTION

Parents teach in the toughest school in the world—the school for making people. . . . There are few schools to train you for your job, and there is no general agreement on the curriculum. You have to make it up yourself. Your school has no holidays, no vacations, no unions, no automatic promotions or pay raises. You are on duty or at least on call 24 hours a day, 365 days a year for at least 18 years for each child you have.

I regard this as the hardest, most complicated, anxiety-ridden sweat-and-blood-producing job in the world. It requires the ultimate in patience, common sense, commitment, humor, tact, love, wisdom, awareness, and knowledge. At the same time, it holds the possibility for the most rewarding, joyous experience of a lifetime.*

What happens when a child enters the family? Are we prepared for the changes that take place in our lives and for the increased responsibility? If it is the first child, new parents may have considered the months of pregnancy and the actual birth of the child to have been the most difficult period only to be surprised to discover how helpless and how demanding a newborn can be.

*Adapted from Virginia Satir, *Peoplemaking* (Palo Alto, California: Science and Behavior Books, Inc., 1972).

1

They may resent the disruption from their careers, social life, and sexual life. They may be alarmed at the cost of a baby and wonder how the bills are going to be paid.

A young baby, toddler, or preschooler takes a lot of parents' time and energy, getting into everything, being stubborn at times, and generally creating a variety of problems for parents to deal with. In some families, the isolation of being at home with the young child is a problem for the young mother who may be far from her family and friends or for the father who may feel neglected or may not know how to relate to a very young baby. Many parents today have not been part of a large family where they had the opportunity to have extended contact with young children and to care for them.

In other cases, parents recognize that the world has changed and want to raise their own children in a way that differs rather significantly from the way they were raised, yet they find themselves falling into familiar patterns or are unsure about which direction to take. They do not always feel competent and would like to be better informed. Child-rearing advice does pour in from many sources. There are books available on how to talk with children, how to discipline them, how to modify their behavior, and how to be an effective parent. Advice columns appear in the daily newspaper and in popular magazines, even those that were formerly devoted to decorating and recipes. How does a parent know which advice to follow?

Our point of view is that there is no sure-fire or easy method of raising children, especially in today's complex and ever-changing society. Certain children are simply easier to raise than others. Then there are the many other factors that impinge on children and their families during the course of their development—for example, economic conditions, social conditions, schooling, the arrival of other children. They, too, have to be considered.

But while the task of parenting may be more difficult than it has been in the past, in many respects it offers a great potential for growth for both parents and children.

Like modern psychological theorists, we take a positive view of development and focus on the potential for growth that exists within all people. Psychological growth is a gradual process that leads to an expanded awareness and is accompanied by a sense of personal freedom to develop, to explore, and to create. In the case of the child, we are beginning with a rather helpless creature who soon responds to the environment and to the developmental forces within by learning to recognize, remember, coordinate actions, and speak. The rate of development in the first five years is quite remarkable. You can see for yourself how mobility, language development, and reasoning gradually allow a child to become more independent. But as powerful as the natural force for the growth of human potential is, it does not take place without some outside assistance. By assistance, we do not mean that a child can be made to grow whether he likes it or not. It is not a passive process which can be done for him or to him. Children themselves are a major factor in determining how they will develop. And although this point of view is optimistic, it does not assume that all will be smooth sailing. In fact, to the extent that growth implies change, it may be expected to disturb the balance of things at times. You and your child are likely to experience periodic states of discomfort as higher states of balance are achieved. Parents and children cannot expect to be always happy; nor should they feel that unhappiness is necessarily a sign of failure.

Being a parent in this process does not mean that you must give up all other areas of satisfaction in your life. Actually, parents who preserve a portion of their lives for themselves and their relationships with other adults are doing both their children and themselves a service. Total devotion to the parenting process is not ideal.

A child grows up and in the process requires more and more freedom to explore and discover, to make mistakes and try again. If you are not too committed to perfection or to having everything turn out your way, you will be more relaxed and will enjoy the process. Facilitating growth can be an arduous task at times and does require caring and patience, flexibility and the ability to own up to your own mistakes. But helping your child grow also gives you the opportunity to grow through interaction with another human being; and it can turn out to be the most exciting and rewarding task you have ever undertaken (when it is not the most frustrating).

chapter two
HAVING A PLAN

Raising a child may be compared with taking a trip. You can make the journey without a map. However, if you choose to do so, the risk of losing your way is considerably greater than if you have some direction or chart of how to reach your destination. Of course, even if you have a plan and a map, an *overcommitment* to a charted course may be as risky as having no plan at all.

We don't want to push this analogy too far. Charting a human life, especially one that is not our own, needs to remain flexible and allow for the inevitable "rerouting" and even rather dramatic changes in direction, if necessary. We are suggesting that following a plan which is subject to modification as the journey proceeds is preferable to embarking on this very important journey without much thought to how you might proceed.

Historically this may not have been as necessary for each parent to do as it is today. There was a time when the direction one might take in raising a child was largely predetermined—there was only one road. Religion and other traditions—national customs and family influences, for example—informed parents rather specifically of what a "good" adult (citizen) was like and how to create that end product of their children. If parents or their children lost their way, there was plenty of support from relatives, community members, and clergymen to remind them of the route to take and to point them in "the proper direction."

Traditional forces such as religion and national customs play a less important role now than they were apt to do in the past. Additional factors have complicated the task of child rearing today and have made it necessary for parents to assume an active decision-making role.

INCREASED OPTIONS

Some parents have more options today than ever before. One example is the increased mobility of individuals and families. Parents may choose to move to another community in order to pursue a business, professional, or educational opportunity. A second example which has had a profound effect upon families is the increased opportunity for women to pursue careers outside the home. These options seem to point to the importance of having a plan, even a tentative one, when you raise a child.

Technology and Change

Much of what was formerly done by humans has now been mechanized. New possibilities in manufacturing, medicine, and virtually every aspect of modern life are constantly being revealed. Change is glorified in advertising, in fashion, in customs, and in music. At the same time, tradition, which formerly served to prevent or retard change, now has a diminished impact on human behavior.

Enhancement of Human Potential

American parents seem to be particularly concerned with the idealistic goal of developing the full and unique potential of their children. Many parents' concern for their children no longer focuses exclusively on the goal of getting a good job in terms of security or making a good marriage. These days parents are likely to be attempting to help each of their children to realize his or her potential as an individual.

Increased Life Span

Living a longer life results in the possibility that individuals will be committed to marriage and occupations for longer periods than was generally the case historically. On the other hand, it also increases the possibility of having several careers and even several marriages within a single lifetime.

YOUR OWN PLAN

Can you raise a child without a plan? Some parents do, of course, for a variety of reasons. Some parents do not know how or what to do. Others have a misguided notion that economic security is equivalent to parenting. Still others think that biological development assures psychological development, which it does not. Then, too, there are parents who choose to raise their children without a plan out of self-interest. Parenting takes work and does require your personal time and energy and the disruption of your routines.

We favor plans, as we note throughout the book, plans that allow for spontaneous change and flexibility related to a child's growth and development, your values, and your growth and development. How do you formulate a plan? There is, after all, so much advice around. How can you sort out these suggestions and apply them to your own child in your own situation?

Keeping in mind our travel metaphor, you can't send to the AAA for a "trip ticket" which maps out a precise route—although some parents attempt to do this when they ritualistically follow the advice of experts. Ultimately, the child-rearing plans you adopt should reflect your own values and, of course, the particular needs of your child. In addition, your plans should be based upon sound developmental principles which enable your child to acquire the ability to function at an optimal level in today's world and in the future. Let's take a look at how developmental principles may be applied to planning for your child.

DEVELOPMENTAL PRINCIPLES

The human child takes longer to grow into maturity than is the case with any other species. This means that human babies are dependent longer than babies born to animal parents. Have you noticed how quickly the offspring of pets you may have had seem to mature? Gerbil babies born without hair and with eyes closed are toddling around in a few days. Within a few weeks they have tripled in size, have a furry coat, and are beginning to see. Within a few months they are fully grown. After an initial brief period of dependency, baby kittens are walking around, can eat solid food, seem to be remarkably well coordinated, and are virtually independent of their parents. Did their parents need to plan their experiences or teach them? It seems that most of their growth and even the interaction between parent and child are "built in" to the developmental program. Human development is less built-in and takes place more slowly.

Yet, even though the human baby seems quite helpless and slow to develop compared with other animals in the beginning, a very substantial amount of intellectual, emotional, and physical growth takes place in the first three years of life. What are the implications of this initial dependency and later rapid growth in motor skills, language, intellectual, and social-emotional development for planning the early experience of children?

In the next chapter, we shall deal more extensively with development. At this point, to demonstrate its relevance for child rearing, let's take a few examples.

Early Stimulation

Many psychologists and educators have observed that young children and even infants are capable of learning. Burton White, for example, has shown that infants who are just a few weeks old respond to interesting visual stimuli when they are placed within view. He also noted that when exposed to these visual stimuli, infants learn to fix their gaze, can track or follow a moving object, and are generally more alert and responsive than infants who are not stimulated in this way. This suggests that while the complexity of human development necessitates a relatively long period of growth, this process may be facilitated and even maximized by our practices as parents and teachers.

If you feel that it is sufficient to provide a new baby with clean sheets, clean diapers, and milk, then you are concentrating only on the physical well-being of the child. If you add to this adult contacts in the form of holding, stroking, and rocking, you are contributing to the child's emotional well-being, too. If you also talk to the child, play peek-a-boo, introduce toys and mobiles, and are generally conscious of the stimuli that encourage reaching, grasping, and looking, you have gone beyond the basics to include a conscious attempt to stimulate intellectual development.

Must you do all the above to be a good parent to an infant? Not necessarily. We are simply saying here that the role of early stimulation and development should be taken into account in planning for your child. Having other small children to care for may influence your decision regarding the amount of time you can spend in the process, but even a relatively well endowed child who is well cared for in a physical sense can profit from specific stimulation from parents in order to encourage intellectual growth in the early years.

Dependency

Erik Erikson has described this early period of development as a conflict between a child's security needs and a fear of loss of support (trust vs. mistrust). The human infant is quite helpless. It is ironic that the infant and the young child both require satisfaction of her dependent needs in order to achieve a genuine sense of independence. The child who feels trusting is more able than a fearful child to explore, to learn, and even to challenge authority when it is necessary to take an initiative. Knowing this, we may wish to satisfy a young child's dependency needs, recognizing that in the long run this may lead to an ability to be independent. If our goal is independence training for our child, we must take into account the appropriate requirement for early emotional and physical support as the child strives naturally and gradually toward independence. Learning theorists would add to this the need to encourage the child's independence by making opportunities for these experiences available and to see wherever possible that they meet with success (reinforcement). This approach tends to lead to a more active intervention on a parent's part.

Autonomy

Autonomy is an important developmental need of children. It is that early desire that children usually demonstrate to do things *their* way, or by themselves, or just not do it at all. This behavior eventually leads to the child's acquiring a sense of self-determination. Erikson points out that a child who struggles for autonomy may end up feeling a sense of shame or guilt about the struggle if parents and other adults are too unwilling to relinquish their control and make her feel like a "bad" child. Admittedly, a two-year-old who says no to everything and has difficulty with toilet training or accepting limits is hard to live with. Yet you may derive some comfort in knowing that her frequent disagreeable behavior is part of the child's natural experiment with self-determination.

An understanding of this developmental need may enable you to allow a child more choice and somewhat more opportunity to say no on occasion without a bitter struggle. What this means is that the child gets to feel some sense of autonomy without losing her sense of security and gains a feeling of acceptance of independence from you. This is a very positive developmental outcome.

Personal Values

A second major determinant of your child-rearing attitudes as well as your goals is, of course, your own values. Sometimes you have these values very clearly in mind as you make decisions. More often than not, however, the values are implicit; that is, they affect your behavior without your being aware of them. While you may not be able to examine every one of the under-lying values that determine how you behave toward your child, it is helpful to take a close look, periodically, at what you are doing and how it may relate to the values which you may feel are important. You may discover, for example, that you are placing more value on cleanliness than on creativity as you insist that a child not get messy, or that you are placing more value on compliance than on training for decision making as you insist that your child do what you say without question.

We are not disparaging the qualities of cleanliness and obedience. We are simply offering the caution that a young child who is taught to be highly compliant and who shows an undue concern about making a mess may not be one who is able to try new things and have a flexibility and openness to new experi-ence, characteristics we view as valuable assets in today's world. In other words, it is helpful to know what values you are giving priority to when you are behaving in a certain way. This is not only useful to the child in terms of your consistency and your plan for the child's future development, but also in terms of your understanding of yourself. At a later point we'll discuss in more detail how your experiences with your child can enable you to learn a great deal about yourself, which is helpful to you as well as to your child.

Society's Needs

Even as we are concerned about the development of an indi-vidual child's potential and how our own personal values and attitudes affect this process, we must finally look beyond the needs of our own individual children and even our own families.

At the most practical level, and as we have sadly observed in our cities, our own children and families are not safe as long as other citizens are starving, emotionally disturbed, angry, or in other ways seriously underprivileged. On a more humane level, it is an important step in the growth of children when they are able to move beyond themselves to begin to consider the needs and point of view of others. An ultimate step is taken when the individual is able to accept his or her place in humanity and to recognize a relation to all people.

The task of preparing citizens of the future has significant implications for your own children's future as well as for the future of society itself. Historically, parents prepared their children to take their place in society by shaping them into the mold required to preserve that society. Tradition, nationalistic spirit, religion, and even etiquette dictated the fashioning of adults of the future. Now we are more likely to be concerned about the individual needs and personal development of our children; but at the same time we have to be concerned with the needs of society in this process, to continue, rebuild, or even change it. Preparing our children for the future necessarily involves a consideration of the qualities needed by our children to create a society which we feel is optimal for the survival and growth of human beings in the future. It works both ways—our children are affected by society, but they also have the potential, individually and collectively, to shape the society in which they live.

QUALITIES FOR THE FUTURE

It would be presumptuous of us to enumerate all the qualities which might be useful for the citizen of the future to have. Qualities will certainly vary from person to person. However, we will show you how we generate our own list of important qualities for children to have and how you may create your own list. Remember, we began this discussion with children's needs and parents' personal values. Now we are examining the characteristics that a child may need as he develops into an effective human being in order to deal with societal issues.

Flexibility

This seems to us to be a more essential quality to develop in children than ever before. The principal reason for this is—

change. As Alvin Toffler has documented in his startling book, *Future Shock,* change is occurring in every aspect of our lives at an accelerated pace. A great deal of this is technological. Most of the inventions upon which we depend today, such as electrical appliances, automobiles, and TV, were not even in existence at the turn of this century. Customs, life styles, types of jobs, and just about anything you can think of has undergone dramatic changes even within the last decade. Parents often find themselves learning about the latest music, style of dress, and language from their children. Obviously, the citizen of the future must be able to adjust to this rapid change without losing identity as a person or feeling overwhelmed. Flexibility, rather than a rigid adherence to past practices, is required to deal with the phenomenon of change. Flexibility is also a useful quality for dealing with other societal trends, such as the lessening of religious, community, and family influence that once offered prescribed ways of behaving. Also, the citizen of today and the future has to deal with the increased mobility of families and individuals. Individuals frequently do not live in the same town or even area where they grew up. Families may relocate several times in the course of the children's development, requiring new friends, adjusting to new schools, learning new customs, and so on.

A Spirit of Cooperation

The complexity of technology has made it increasingly necessary for a product or even a service to be produced or delivered by more than one individual. Our dependence upon one another for goods and services and work has increased markedly from the earliest days of our country and is continuing at an accelerated pace. Even the institution of the American farm family that was almost self-sufficient has given way to the need for a more complex system of survival. Our dependence upon governmental services in the form of military, police, and fire protection has expanded to the areas of education, welfare, consumer and environmental protection, and others. What does this mean in terms of the human qualities needed for survival?

Modern society has placed an emphasis on helping children to break away from traditional constraints and to develop autonomy and self-direction. While these individual needs may require that a child resist sharing and other cooperative efforts at times, children must also learn to recognize and to accept their relationship to others. Children learn about reciprocal relationships in their family as they move from an egocentric state to a sociocentric one. In this process the children acquire an ability to take the perspective of others and achieve a sense of belonging as they discover their common bond with others. There is a "natural" development, but it is dependent upon environmental facilitation. It is a quality to be encouraged and nurtured if we are going to be able to survive as a society of mutually interdependent people.

Autonomy and Self-Direction

There are many forces in the modern world that seem to conspire against an individual's feeling of self-worth. It is often difficult to achieve a feeling of personal effectiveness in a complicated world that is not always responsive to our personal needs. The demands for cooperative efforts and the rapid changes which we've just described may at times undermine our self-confidence and our willingness to fight to preserve our self-direction. Again, children strive naturally for autonomy in the earliest stages of development. The reactions of parents and teachers to young children's desires to do things for themselves, to resist direction, and to explore have important implications for the older children's and adults' abilities for self-determination. Some children submit passively or appear indifferent. Others · distort this need into a stubborn refusal to take any advice or to cooperate in any way. Clearly, these are not desirable outcomes. Even if an adult has learned to accommodate to the requirements of society, it is useful to be able to withstand community pressures at some point and to proceed in a direction which may not be popular or fashionable. We would like to prepare our children to be able to be self-determined when necessary.

The Ability to Enjoy Solitude

Here we've chosen a somewhat less obvious quality to cultivate in children but nevertheless one which we feel is especially important in light of the increasing demands of society to be part of a group. Parents have often discussed with us their concern that their children do not have many friends or even prefer to be alone. In today's society, not being popular is often viewed as a cause for alarm, but is it necessarily a disability? Conditions such as overcrowding, complexity, and the need for working together do place great pressure on mastery of techniques for getting along well with others. This is compounded by the rapid changes in customs and tasks which often turn people to one another to discover how to dress and how to act. David Riesman, the sociologist, calls this being "other-directed." Still, we need a sense of ourselves, too, and at times this requires an ability to move away from the crowd and to work and reflect in a more solitary situation. Many young people seem to be losing this ability and, as a result, have become too dependent upon others for direction. Obviously, some kind of balance is needed whereby an individual has both the flexibility and openness to see others' points of view and to cooperate in collective efforts and at the same time the ability to tolerate temporary states of aloneness as she withdraws to think or to work.

The examples in this chapter of how to use the three bases (the child, your values, society) for decision making in parenting are not all-inclusive. They are offered as guidelines for your consideration as you formulate your own plan for raising children. Remember, too, the importance of "mapping" a flexible route as you attempt to set a course for you and your children.

ADDITIONAL READING

ERIKSON, ERIK, *Childhood and Society*. New York: Norton, 1950.
NIXON, ROBERT, *The Art of Growing*. New York: Random House, 1962.

RIESMAN, DAVID, WITH GLAZER, NATHAN, AND DENNY, REVEL, *The Lonely Crowd.* New Haven, Connecticut: Yale University Press, 1950.

TOFFLER, ALVIN, *Future Shock.* New York: Random House, 1970.

WHITE, BURTON, *The First Three Years of Life.* Englewood Cliffs, N.J.: Prentice-Hall, 1975.

chapter three
HOW DOES YOUR CHILD GROW?

In the last chapter we talked about having a plan. It is very important to take into account the child himself when you are thinking about your plan for him. This involves two essential elements: theories of development and individual differences. In this chapter we shall discuss how you can coordinate your ideas about raising children, your goals for your child, and the child's own rate of development and personality. Let's begin by looking at two hypothetical infants, Ralph and Sally.

Ralph was born after a rather easy delivery. Labor lasted less than an hour. He weighed eight pounds two ounces at birth. His mother had to be sedated, so she was not awake enough to see him until five hours after delivery, when he was brought to her room. Ralph was a "quiet" baby who slept a great deal. He enjoyed eating, but he never seemed to be satisfied. His major signs of distress occurred when he was hungry. He could be comforted by contact, although he was very demanding in this area, too. He babbled early and was saying words by one year. In his second year he spoke in sentences. Ralph was not very agile or active in the physical area.

Sally's delivery was by natural childbirth. She weighed six pounds fourteen ounces. Delivery went smoothly, but labor lasted eleven hours. Her mother was allowed to hold her close on her body for about one-half hour after birth while her father looked on proudly. The father had been at his wife's side during the long labor period. When her mother saw her later, after mother and daughter had had a chance to rest, she noticed that Sally moved a great deal more than she had imagined an infant could. Sally did not seem to like to be held too tightly, which was a bit disappointing to her mother, who wanted to cuddle her. Instead, Sally preferred to move her limbs and to look around. She did not like to stay still. She continued to be an active child. In fact, at eight months her parents had difficulty keeping her in her crib, and by twelve months she really resisted staying in a playpen.

As you can see, Ralph and Sally seem to be very different from each other at birth, and the differences persisted through infancy and early childhood. To what extent are these differences "built in" biologically? We can't tell exactly. The children do have different temperaments. Ralph likes to take things easy, while Sally prefers to be up and doing. This makes a difference in how they are treated of course, which in turn affects their personalities. But what is behind that? They are different genetically. They inherited certain characteristics, including aspects of their temperament, from their parents. Ralph's parents are relatively sedate; they prefer quiet activites, require lots of sleep, and are not athletic. We might suspect that this is an inherited trait, since it was evident in the child at birth and is consistent with his parents' temperament. It might also be possible that this preference was learned, since Ralph's sedentary nature was encouraged by his parents, who found the compatibility comfortable and who also provided an example of slow-paced adults for Ralph to imitate.

What about Sally? She is more active than Ralph, but it seems less likely that this is an inherited characteristic because her parents are slow-paced. In fact, they do not encourage Sally's behavior, which they compare to a whirlwind. Perhaps if they were more active themselves they would appreciate her get-up-and-go quality. In any case, where did such an active temperament come from? Again, it would be difficult to say exactly. Babies have a prenatal history during which they are affected by the mother's diet, drugs she might take (including nicotine), and her emotional state. They are also affected by the birth process itself, labor and delivery. In Sally's case, her mother had been very apprehensive during most of the period of pregnancy. She was looking forward to motherhood, but she was worried about finances, since she wasn't planning to work. She was also concerned about how her husband would adjust to the change in their life style and the attention she would need to give to the infant. She thought that getting him involved in natural childbirth would help him to feel closer to the process. This plan seemed to work eventually, but in the first stages of her pregnancy he was not very supportive, which added to her anxiety. The adrenaline and other bodily chemicals associated with her anxiety were transmitted to the fetus through her bloodstream and may have contributed to the baby's high activity level. One couldn't say for sure at this point; we do know that the baby's birth and delivery were not particularly traumatic. Sally could also have inherited her active temperament, because inherited characteristics are not always apparent in parents, although they are passed on to children. Such traits are called "recessive" and may skip a generation.

We mentioned earlier that Sally's parents found her need to be on the move to be less compatible with their style of behavior compared with Ralph's parents, who preferred his quiet nature. What we are discovering is that the match between parents and child is a very significant factor in determining how the child is regarded by parents and how, in turn, the child feels about himself. This is sometimes referred to as a reciprocal relationship in that parents are affected by their child's behavior just as, more obviously, their child is affected by how they treat him. Let's look at this reciprocity in our two infants, Sally and Ralph.

Ralph likes to cuddle and is affectionate. He was also an early talker. These qualities are enjoyed by his parents. You might say that these qualities are rewarding to them as they care for Ralph. Ralph's personality makes his parents' job more pleasant, although the demanding nature of his eating and his need for parent contact could be a problem for some parents. Sally's parents have a somewhat harder time, since, as we've said, she tends to be more active than they would prefer. Also, Sally is described as not being very cuddly. Perhaps she doesn't like being confined. In any case, her parents don't get the satisfaction of being able to hold her close. They might even feel, sometimes, that she is too independent for her age, so they are disappointed. Of course, not all parents prefer their babies cuddly; in some cases, they themselves are not physically affectionate.

What satisfactions can be gained from a baby like Sally? Actually, there are many. Her parents may learn to appreciate her physical agility, her curiosity, and her vitality. If you were Sally's parent, how would you feel about her? Would you be able to enjoy her? It is valuable, as a parent, to take note of your child's style of behavior and preferences. Even though they may not be entirely compatible with yours, you should attempt to see their positive aspects. As you react favorably to your child's positive attributes, you will be helping him to view himself positively and are also likely to find that you will enjoy your child more, too.

INDIVIDUAL DIFFERENCES

As our example above attempted to demonstrate, there is quite a significant difference between children, even at birth. If you have more than one child, you know from firsthand experience that each child has a unique personality. This includes how a child reacts to change, how affectionate he is, how visual, how verbal, how active, how irritable, and so forth. How do you, as a parent, take this into account?

Most generally, it helps not to expect the same thing from each child. You might have expectations from a previous child or from your own experiences as a child; you may hope that your child will be athletic or beautiful or affectionate. You might only be comparing your child to a hypothetical case, but in any event, you are likely to be disappointed because few children fulfill these expectations exactly. On the other hand, if you look at your child as unique, an individual who has his own special qualities, you may be pleasantly surprised. You can get to know your baby's style, his preferences, his way of reacting even when he is an infant, if you are observant. You may learn that he doesn't require as much sleep as other infants or that he doesn't like too much cuddling. You might help him to become a better eater or to be more cuddly, but it is not advisable to attempt to get a child to give up his own individuality to become what you wish him to be. You'll find that if you support your child's strengths he will feel better about himself, and, in the long run, he may be more willing to try to develop skills and other qualities which may not come as easily to him. The important difference is that he will be doing so because he feels capable, not because he feels he has no choice.

THE DEVELOPMENTAL POINT OF VIEW

Although your child's personality may be modified somewhat and expressed differently as he grows older, most of the underlying qualities will remain the same. If he is slow to react, for example, or doesn't take well to change, this will remain more or less characteristic of him throughout life. This is a form of continuity, sort of like a "psychological fingerprint."

The changes that you will observe in your child over time are accounted for by two principal factors: learning and development. The former is mostly a product of his environment, while the latter is more closely related to the biological changes that take place as he grows. Yet, these environmental and biological changes are not completely independent of one another. The biological changes, including physical size and agility, are affected by environmental factors such as nutrition and exercise, while learning is dependent upon the biological readiness of the child.

The developmental point of view takes into account the fact that children are different intellectually and emotionally, as well as physically, at different stages in their lives. The physical changes are usually the most easily observable and, therefore, the most obvious. But as we have noted previously, the way children look at things, their perspective, how they process information, their thinking, their emotional needs, and how they feel about their experiences also change as they develop. All of these changes on their part require adjustments on your part. Just when you think you have a good idea of what to expect, you need to make some new adjustments.

A common example of developmental change is the child's need for dependence. Infants and children under age two generally have the most pronounced need in this area. They can do relatively little to care for themselves; their first priority is to be cared for by someone else. However, once they acquire speech and locomotion, their independence is increased. At that stage, they begin to say no more frequently, and they try to do more for themselves. Their autonomy needs begin to receive more priority.

There was a time when children were generally viewed as "miniature adults." While most parents today recognize that their children may have different priorities, different ways of thinking, and a different point of view than they do, it is difficult to keep this in mind in your actual daily dealings with your child. After all, you have your own priorities and expectations as a parent. Perhaps you would like your child to be well-mannered or to be able to share well or to be able to understand why you may not have been able to keep your "promise" on occasion. If you have an understanding of development, you may be able to recognize that your child's inability to live up to your expectations may be, in fact, appropriate for his age. This should lessen your disappointment somewhat and allow you to be more accepting of his behavior at this developmental level.

We won't be able to review all of the developmental characteristics that are typical of young children here, but we will discuss a number of significant ones that you may be able to identify in your own child. To make these developmental principles easier to apply, we have divided them into three areas: physical needs, learning and thinking, and emotional characteristics. Let's first take a look at *infants*.

INFANTS

The Feeding Process

It is clear that no two infants are exactly alike physically, even identical twins. There are certain basic physical needs that characterize most infants' behavior.

One basic need state for all infants is hunger. As we attempted to show in the example above, there is considerable variation in children here. Some babies are very hungry and demanding, while others are better able to withstand delay of feeding. This need is basic to survival, of course, but it also affects the relationship between parent and child. From the child's point of view, it is best to "tune in" to the amount of food and the feeding schedule that best suit his needs. From your own point of view, you also need to socialize your child to a waking, sleeping, and feeding pattern that conforms somewhat to your own schedule. This really is a question of balance or, what we've called before, *reciprocity*. If, at first, you are flexible with your infant as you "tune in" to his needs, you can gently help move him in a particular direction. It is no more advisable to allow your infant to dominate you by requiring that you conform to an irregular or too-frequent feeding schedule than it is for you to expect him to have three meals a day at the conventional times.

There has been considerable research done on the advisability of breast or bottle feeding. We will not repeat all of the arguments pro and con here. We wish to emphasize that there are both physical and emotional components involved in the feeding process. A mother who bottle-feeds her baby and one who breast-feeds hers can each hold and relate to her child in a close way. However you choose to feed your infant, be flexible and do not take personally the difficulty he may be having in accepting food. What starts out as a primary physical need can become an emotional problem or an asset to a child depending how it is handled; some children make it easier than others by being easy to feed and by being good eaters.

Kinesthetic Stimulation—
The Importance of Body Contact

Let's take a look at another attribute of infants that begins as a physical need but also has important implications for the child's emotional well-being. Infants generally appear to have a need for close bodily contact. A psychologist named Harry Harlow made an extensive study of the "kinesthetic" need in infant chimps, animals who are close relatives of humans. He discovered that infant chimps preferred to be with soft, cuddly mothers even more than being with the mothers who fed them. He also learned that in time of stress, the mothers who were soft and cuddly were able to provide security to the chimps while the less soft ones were not. What does this mean for human babies? It strongly suggests that the physical contact that you provide your infant through handling is naturally comforting to him and will also provide him with a sense of security which will enable him to explore the world around him at a later period. You don't really need to make special time for holding your baby. You simply have to be aware that as you feed and change him and otherwise attend to his physical needs, it is good to hold him close and to stroke him. You are extending the time that you normally interact with him and making the most of the time that you do have together. As an extra treat for you as well as him, you might find time to rock with him. For most babies, this provides pleasure (it is also good for digestion and respiration) along with the close contact that he needs.

Visual Stimulation—
The Infant Likes to Look

Infants require a certain amount of stimulation to develop their competence. A baby who is isolated from sights and sounds and is rarely handled is not likely to prosper physically, emotionally, or intellectually. Newborns are much more aware of stimulation, visual and otherwise, than was once thought to be the case. Research has demonstrated that infants who find their world attractive and stimulating tend to reach out for it with their eyes and their hands. It is as if nature needs an additional ingredient to bring out the best in the unfolding child.

Infants also respond to the human face as a stimulus quite naturally and readily, even before they get to know whose it is. This is another natural mechanism that increases the chances of an infant's survival. If you respond to this natural interest on his part by being available and rewarding to him, his tendency to seek human contact is enhanced, and the beginning of social conditioning takes place. Bending close while talking gently will likely cause the baby to become animated and even to reciprocate a bit. Peek-a-boo games are fun and helpful to the developing child. They help to teach about constancy and to relieve possible anxieties about loss, which are very much a part of a young child's life.

The infant is not interested exclusively in eating and sleeping. It is true that he does spend a relatively brief time awake in the first week: two to three hours a day. But by the fourth week, he is already awake on the average of four to five hours per day and needs even more opportunities to look around and to interact with you.

It has been discovered that he likes change and variety in what he sees. Mobiles are very popular. Not only are they visually attractive, but they also offer change and movement. Many people hang mobiles high above an infant. Actually, the infant's vision is limited to what is close at hand—about nine inches from his face. They get more involved with mobiles that are rather close to them in the crib. Don't worry if your infant can eventually reach the mobile with a hand or foot. This is a natural and very desirable extension of his exploration. First he notices things, then he begins to recognize them, and then he begins to touch them; first by accident, then by design.

In his tracking and following attractive objects, he is making his first step forward intellectually. Infant seats are very useful in this regard. They give the child support while allowing him to look around; and they are portable, which means he can observe in different locations. Of course, you have to be vigilant to note when he is beginning to tire. Aside from the possible physical fatigue of being in the upright position, infants can become overstimulated. If lights are too bright or there is too much novelty or too many people to interact with, the infant will react defensively. He will literally "shut down." It is not a good idea for him to have to reach this point too often.

A Sense of "Self" and "Other"

What is happening to a child emotionally during the infancy period? In the first place, he is getting some sense of what other people are like through his interaction with you. Initially he isn't really able to tell where he ends and you begin. Sigmund Freud called this a period of *omnipotence* because the infant may have the feeling that he is responsible for everything that happens to him. As he begins to recognize his dependence on you, he can either be reassured because there is someone big and dependable who cares for him, or he can become frightened if he doesn't find you reliable or senses that you don't like him. He is beginning to form a picture of the outside world and of his place in it. This is not a full-fledged articulated view but more like a positive or negative feeling in the first stages. It can also be changed at a later period, and often is, but it is nevertheless the initial basis of how the child feels about himself and others—safe or insecure, loving or unloving, dependable or undependable. While the effects are not irreversible, this early picture tends to color the rest of his experience and provide the basis for future relationships. So, as you see, these early interactions with your infant are very significant. Caring for your child's physical needs is important, as is gentle handling, cuddling and stroking, and talking to him in a pleasant, loving tone. These are valuable ways to communicate to him about himself and others.

THE TODDLER

Increased Mobility

The toddler is characterized by increased mobility. This is likely to represent some significant changes for him and for you. He has an increased sense of his capacity: he is aware that he can do more. In a normal child, this is accompanied by a desire to use his newly acquired capacities to expand his horizons. But like an experimenter with a new invention, he typically doesn't have things completely under control. He gets into places he could not formerly reach, including, perhaps, your kitchen cabinets, dresser drawers, and other areas which may be dangerous as well as annoying for him to be investigating. This is a dramatic change from the infant whom you could count as as being in one place, even though he wasn't always happy there.

How are you going to react to this change? You might be upset, as we've said, that he is into everything or that he requires more supervision. You might be worried that he will get hurt. From a developmental point of view, it is important to recognize that his increased mobility is a natural development in his maturation. It is important for his physical development for him to move about, but intellectually also he needs to explore what he can do and what is around him. At this stage, he investigates in a concrete way, by touching and feeling and even tasting. Emotionally, he should have a feeling of security to explore in this way. This leads to a feeling of competence and a beginning of trusting himself.

What is your part in this? Of course you can't allow him to go wherever he wants and to explore everything. You need to set limits. But these boundaries should be reasonable and provide him with some space. Perhaps you can let him play with pots which you deliberately place in the lower cabinets. You may have to remove dangerous cleaning agents or sharp objects to higher places or to locked storage. You can make certain rooms off-limits, but don't be surprised if he tests you or doesn't really remember at first. To help, you may have to lock or barricade certain rooms to start and then gradually remove the barriers as you feel he understands. You also should select playthings which can contribute to your child's intellectual growth, such as plastic containers for sorting, stacking, and putting things in, as well as puzzles and blocks.

Beginning Verbal Skills:
"No" and "Why"

The toddler is experimenting with language much the same as he is experimenting with getting around. He is trying out a new skill. How does it work? Do people listen? Are they pleased? Do they encourage him or do they ignore him or tell him to shut up? Perhaps he is keeping a new baby awake. He may be repeating himself a lot. That is natural for someone trying out a new skill. It is important to encourage this burgeoning speech, of course. It is likely to require some patience on your part, as well as support. When a child first speaks, he tends to use one-word sentences. These are not always easy to understand. For example, if he says "milk," you have to determine if he means "I am thirsty" or "I see the milk" or is merely practicing a new word. You can usually get the meaning from the context if you are patient. Another form of patience testing for parents is the toddler's tendency to use words to get attention. That is the reason behind the repeated "why's" that come in a series. Your answer serves as a reinforcement for the next "why," so it goes on for a long time. If you wish to encourage language, you need to put up with this experiment that goes "If I say a particular word (perhaps 'mommy'), will I get an answer?" It gives the child, among other things, a sense of competence to be able to get you to react in this way and, of course, a sense of power, too.

Speaking of a sense of power, children at this age (about two years) have a tendency to say "no" a great deal and to refuse to do things. Hence the nickname "the terrible two's." We know that that kind of behavior is hard to take at times. What is it all about? Part of what is happening is what we described above, an experiment with language. But the fixation on "no" suggests that the child is beginning to express verbally a resistance that represents the first stages of autonomy—being one's own person.

Obviously, this negativism at age two is not easy to take as a parent, especially since it is often so apparently unreasonable. Children at this age are likely to refuse even something that they like. It is best to think of it this way—they are merely asserting their right to say no. It is, after all, about the only power they have at this age—the power of resistance. Some children exercise this power more than others. Clearly, you can't always give in to this refusal. But it is important that you allow your child to refuse sometimes when possible. When you can't give in, it helps to offer an explanation. "Today it is cold. We need to wear hats." This brief explanation eventually develops meaning for the child.

THE PRESCHOOL CHILD

For discussion purposes, we shall divide the developmental milestones that characterize this period into three areas: physical needs, learning and thinking, and emotional needs. As was the case with infants and toddlers, these areas overlap considerably. For example, a physical characteristic, such as eye-hand coordination, can have significant implications for learning and intellectual development while it may also contribute to a child's emotional well-being. Yet psychologists and educators have traditionally made these three distinctions in order to examine the contribution of each area more closely, as we'll be doing here.

Physical Needs

YOUNG CHILDREN ARE ACTIVE.   While there is individual variation, young children are generally characterized as active. Now that they have gone beyond the toddler stage, they are better able to get around. This may become a problem for you as they move from room to room or outdoors or because they are noisy or always seem to be looking for something to do. A young child can't really be expected to sit still for long periods of time, although he may do so when engrossed in a task. Movement is usually part of a child's nature; even if he is standing or sitting still, his arms and legs are likely to be going. You may find this distracting, and, of course, you can encourage the child to sit or stand less actively, but you will have more success if you can put that energy to work. Here's an example:

> The Jones family is waiting for dinner to be served at a restaurant. Tommy, age four, is very restless. Mrs. Jones had thought ahead. She hands Tommy a pencil and some paper to draw. He works on his drawing and discusses it with the family.

Getting your young child involved constructively by helping you to set the table at home or playing a game in a restaurant while waiting for the food to be served is clearly more desirable than yelling at him to keep still.

When your child is moving around as he plays in the house or yard, you may not always be able or inclined to follow him around, although that's good to do sometimes, since he is likely to enjoy the attention and needs the supervision. It is easier on you and fun for him if you can provide him some space with his toys or even some pots and pans and let him explore on his own. You may be able to do your own work or relax in a nearby room where you can see him and he can see you. Then, if he needs help, you can serve as a "consultant" or "helper," being careful not to take over. Burton White, in his research, has found that mothers who are nearby to serve as consultants in this way generally have the most competent children.

YOUNG CHILDREN LIKE TO EXPLORE.   This period is one of the most exploring times in a child's life. Erikson calls it a time of "initiative." Increased mobility and a preliminary sense of autonomy allow your child to move forward by taking a closer look at things. Children at this age like to experiment with materials such as paint, water, and clay. They are also curious about how things work and what is inside things. This exploratory need is demonstrated in physical activity, but as we mentioned previously, it contributes to the growth of intelligence and also allows the child to acquire a sense of competence as he begins to learn about his environment and his place in it.

The combination of high activity and a desire to explore can, as we have noted, create a problem for you as a parent.

Certainly, a young child's tendency to touch everything, take things apart, and play with things that may be unsafe or inappropriate can be annoying as well as dangerous. How do you strike a balance between encouraging active exploration and setting appropriate limits? This is not always easy. We have found that the most positive solution is providing acceptable materials and opportunities for active exploration. We shall be describing some of these in detail in chapters 7 and 9. Your child needs to learn to distinguish between those things and circumstances which allow only visual exploration ("look with your eyes") and those which allow for the more direct touching that a child of this age generally prefers. Try to avoid imposing too many restrictions. If you find that you are saying "don't touch" or "stay away" too often, you should think about redesigning your child's living and playing area so that he is not as much in contact with things he shouldn't be playing with. Equipment such as record players and tape recorders may present a problem. Children can use them alone, if they are sturdy ones. If you have a delicate or expensive piece of equipment, it should be stored out of reach until you are available. Even if you've let your child use it under supervision, he is likely to try it if it is available when you aren't around.

YOUNG CHILDREN'S FINE MOTOR SKILLS GENERALLY DEVELOP MORE SLOWLY THAN THEIR LARGE MOTOR SKILLS.   Young children are gaining control over all aspects of their motor coordination as they grow, but it is helpful to realize that the muscles in their fingers are a bit more difficult to bring under control than the muscles in their upper arms. This developmental trend means that you should not expect your young child to be adept at activities that require precise dexterity, such as buttoning or zippering or cutting with scissors. Less fine motor skills, such as running and jumping, usually are easier, since they generally develop earlier.

Activities such as bead stringing, Lego, block building, and playing with puzzles help a child to develop his small motor skills, but the beads, blocks, and puzzle pieces should be large enough so that he is encouraged to work in this area rather than become frustrated by the experience. Observing him while he is doing these activities is a good way to tell what he is ready for. Children differ in this regard, but if yours seems impatient and doesn't stay at the activity long, you might try larger-scale materials. Doing zippers and buttons and putting on socks and other clothing by himself, with some guidance, is also helpful to the child. These activities help to foster dexterity as well as independence.

YOUNG CHILDREN CANNOT WAIT FOR LONG PERIODS AT A TIME. Another physical fact that must be taken into account when planning for your young child is that most children of this age find it very difficult to wait. There are many reasons for this, including their preference for activity, which we discussed earlier. Actually, a major reason for their apparent impatience is intellectual; a young child's subjective sense of time is different from an adult's. It is as if they have a different internal clock. A five-minute wait for you may appear to your child to be more like thirty minutes, which is why he may find it so hard to endure. Still another reason why your child may have a hard time waiting is that the emotional capacity for delaying gratification is less well developed in children than in adults. This may make them appear demanding, but it is a natural characteristic at this age to find it difficult to wait for something that you want very much. We even have this problem as adults on occasion. Yet there are times when your child has to wait. How can you help him accommodate to this situation? Simply avoid unnecessary delays. In many cases, waiting is inevitable, but think of the times you may have told your child to wait a minute while you have taken considerably longer before answering him, or how many times you may have helped him to get dressed to go somewhere and left him waiting. It would be helpful to minimize these delays. Of course, you can't always interrupt what you're doing, but if you keep the child's time clock in mind, you may be able to shorten some times you expect him to wait.

Prepare together whenever possible. If you are baking cookies with your child or doing an art project, get the ingredients ready in advance. You may wish to have your preschooler help you get together the necessary items from around the house before you begin. This way your child does not have to wait in place while you search for scissors or a measuring cup. Generally, if you do a little planning in advance, both you and your child benefit.

YOUNG CHILDREN USUALLY HAVE SHORT ATTENTION SPANS. Don't expect your young child to remain highly involved in an activity for longer than about fifteen minutes. There are exceptions to this, of course, in that sometimes a young child spontaneously gets involved in something for a longer period. Children differ in this regard. The point is not to plan or choose activities that last much longer, especially when your child is looking and listening; this includes bedtime stories or entertainment. Your child might be an exception, but be prepared if you take your child to a movie or read him your favorite fairy tale, that he may lose interest before it's over.

Mental Activities

LEARNING AND THINKING.   A good deal of the child's thinking at this age is done in activity. If you watch your child examining a new toy, material, or household object, you'll observe that he is "looking it over" with his hands as well as his eyes. If he is seeing how a piece of chewed bubble gum stretches or sticks to things, you may not be very pleased, but it may be easier to bear if you think of him as a young scientist experimenting. Swiss psychologist Jean Piaget revolutionized our ideas about children's thinking by looking at it in this way. According to him, they are forming categories in their brains and testing these ideas out against their experience. The more observing and exploring they do, the more they are able to expand and refine their mental categories. Here are four basic ideas about young children's thinking that you may find useful in understanding your child.

YOUNG CHILDREN LEARN FROM THEIR OWN ACTIVITY.   As Piaget and early childhood educators such as Maria Montessori have described, young children learn by doing. They need to get involved with objects physically. They take in information best by having direct contact with it, and they also think and learn in this manner through direct manipulation of the materials. They do not learn as well by having things explained to them, which we as adults may sometimes find difficult to understand. What they learn by direct experience is generally more lasting and meaningful to them. As we said earlier, this means that we should view this activity positively and make provision for it.

YOUNG CHILDREN LEARN FROM DIRECT EXPERIENCE WITH CON-CRETE MATERIALS.   Children learn from touching and holding and manipulating actual objects and materials. For example, they love water and enjoy feeling it and floating and sinking objects in it. Where can they do this without making too much of a mess? An obvious place is the bath. Children like to have extra time for playing at bath time when it's possible. At other times, you might be able to give your child materials to pour and play with at the sink under your supervision.

Children also learn from baking. They love the contact they get as they mix and squeeze the dough. Gardening is another activity that allows for actual use of and contact with materials as they dig in the dirt, weed, and work in the garden.

YOUNG CHILDREN LEARN A GREAT DEAL FROM IMITATION. What you do is likely to have more impact on your child's learning than what you say. Your behavior serves as a concrete representation for your child, and his imitation affords an opportunity for active learning. It is important to be aware of your effect as a model. It sometimes bothers us when our children pick up features that we don't particularly like which they have copied from us. On the other hand, if you show enthusiasm, concern, and courtesy, your child is likely to behave in that way. It doesn't always work, but it is more effective than simply telling them how to behave and then behaving in a different way yourself. By the same token, participate in their activities when you can and when it's appropriate. Try not to dominate, of course, but don't always stand on the sidelines either, or your child will also.

Emotional Characteristics

In a broad sense, a young child's emotional reactions are like those of an adult. He experiences a range of feelings even though he is not able to make subtle distinctions. On the other hand, from an adult point of view, the young child may appear to overreact. He may get very upset about a seemingly minor incident or show extremes of joy or despair rather than a moderate reaction. There are some significant characteristics of children's emotions that you should be aware of in dealing with your young child.

YOUNG CHILDREN ARE EGOCENTRIC. This is true intellectually as well as emotionally. Young children tend to be self-centered. This developmental tendency for a child to see things from his own point of view may make your young child appear selfish and even amoral at times. Young children generally find it difficult if not impossible to see things from another person's point of view. This makes sharing or being sorry or sympathetic—qualities valued by most adults—especially difficult at this age. While you may attempt to help your child to try to think about others, keep in mind that this is not easy and requires some patience on your part; otherwise the child will feel very guilty over rather normal problems with taking another's perspective.

Adults often put great priority on manners, such as saying "I'm sorry" when you've hurt someone else or on being sympathetic to another's distress. Children under seven can learn how to show these overt reactions if they are trained, but they actually have little inner sense of these emotions. It is advisable to remind children about the amenities but to recognize that the genuine feeling isn't likely to come until later. Our formula is not to place too great an emphasis on the formality of saying you're sorry or displaying sympathy, but to remind the child of how his action affects others. For example, you might say, "Your brother doesn't like it when you draw on his books" or "It makes me very happy that you shared your ice cream with me."

Another way to encourage this behavior is by behaving in this manner yourself. As we've said, children learn best by example. If you are courteous and considerate of their needs, that increases the likelihood that they will behave that way, too. Remember, though, that while they may learn to behave in a more courteous and sympathetic manner, their natural egocentricity at this age may make it difficult for them to do this consistently or to take another person's perspective to really understand these feelings.

YOUNG CHILDREN HAVE A NEED FOR AUTONOMY. Some children exhibit this need more obviously than others. Most young children at least experiment with bossy behavior and enjoy being in control at times. This is the same reason why some very insecure adults exhibit bossy and controlling behavior. On the positive side, it provides the child with his first sense of self-direction and a feeling of competency. Of course, bossy and stubborn behavior can be very annoying to you as a parent. While we are pointing out that his form of self-direction and even resistance is healthy at times, parents still need to channel this behavior and to set limits for it. This is another case of your having to help your child find a balance between his own needs and those of others.

The child's need is for autonomy. This is a positive form of independence that goes beyond stubbornness. In a more mature form it should lead to a feeling of being confident in your own judgment. Carl Rogers, a well-known therapist, calls this "trusting yourself." It is a form of inner strength that contributes to a child's willingness to try. How do you help your child achieve a sense of autonomy at this stage in his life when he is, after all, quite dependent on you? One of the best ways is through the offering of choices. This does not mean letting your child do whatever he wants. You will find that he enjoys making limited choices, such as "Would you like a green one or a red one?" At the same time, he is preparing for making choices in the future. He will probably be confused or at least have difficulty if there are too many things to choose from at first, so it is best to provide him with only two choices.

It is also important that you offer your child choices that are realistic. For example, you may not be willing to let him wear everything he picks out for school. He needs to be helped, to learn what is appropriate. You may need to designate some of his clothes "school clothes" so that he may choose different things to wear on a nonschool day. A very unrealistic choice that we notice parents offering children is "Do you want to go now?" What do you do if the child says no? Are you prepared to stay longer? You must ask yourself these questions before you offer this type of choice. You may want to say, "Do you want to go now or in five minutes?" which may be a more realistic choice for him.

It is helpful as a parent to remind yourself that autonomy needs do frequently take the form of resistance at this age. If you keep in mind that your child is really asking "Can I say no?" when he refuses, it may make it somewhat easier to let him do so on occasion. His resistance may also take the form of not being willing to listen to you read him a story when you want to or not wanting to go with you to a wonderful place. But you need to accept this refusal sometimes if he is going to acquire a sense of autonomy.

YOUNG CHILDREN HAVE A NEED FOR DEPENDENCY.   In spite of the fact that your growing child needs to assert his independence, it is important not to overlook the fact that he is equally as likely to seek your help at other times. Sometimes this apparent contradiction is startling. You may feel that he has outgrown his helpless state, but more than likely he will act in a helpless way at times, particularly at times of stress or when he is hurt. Ironically, it may be after he has asserted himself when he seems to need the reassurance that he has not lost your support. So even after he has demonstrated some gains toward independence, don't expect a continual movement in this direction without some occasional lapses. Human growth and development does not proceed evenly.

YOUNG CHILDREN ARE EASILY FRUSTRATED.   There is quite a range even in adults' abilities to tolerate frustration. Some people are very patient, while others get angry and upset easily.

Generally, children are less able to withstand delay, failure, and other disappointments than adults. Infants scream when they are hungry. Hopefully, as they grow older they learn to tolerate not having their needs fulfilled immediately. While your young child should be encouraged to develop capacities for withstanding frustrations, he should not be expected to behave as an adult in this regard.

Needless delays and waits, as we pointed out earlier, are a strain on children, as are tasks that are too delicate or otherwise too difficult for them to perform. Knowing that your young child may find frustration difficult to handle, it is important to select tasks that are not too far "out of reach" for him to do. How can you tell which tasks are likely to be too frustrating? Experience is the best indicator of what he can do and how his patience is holding up. It also helps to keep his age in mind when you choose things for him to do and to think about the dexterity, language, coordination, and memory that the task may require. It is good to try it out yourself beforehand so you can determine where he might need help and, of course, whether it's appropriate for him in the first place.

YOUNG CHILDREN ARE OFTEN FEARFUL.   Young children are, after all, rather vulnerable—especially when they are infants and toddlers. They need to depend on you, or someone else at first, for survival. As they become increasingly self-sufficient, they are still inclined to harbor a host of fears, including the fear of being separated from you, a possible cautiousness in physical activity, or a reluctance to try new things. While these fears may not always appear realistic to you, nonetheless they are normal concerns for children at this age. To take the fear of being separated from you, for example, when your child feels that he's done something bad or that you are displeased with him, he may be reluctant to separate from you. He feels that you may want to get rid of him. Actually, in that case you may indeed be angry with him, which makes it especially hard to have him close by, but ironically this may be the time when he especially needs your reassurance. It is important to take these fears seriously and provide needed reassurance rather than ridicule or attempt to stop him from being afraid or denying that there is anything to be afraid of.

Sometimes we try to make a child feel less afraid by telling him what he is afraid of is "nothing." We might even go further to tell him "You're not afraid" when, in fact, he is. It is important to acknowledge your child's fears because they are usually realistic to him. You might say, for example, "I see that you are scared. Sometimes flies do sound scary, but they don't really hurt us."

YOUNG CHILDREN NEED TO FEEL COMPETENT.   Perhaps the most important feeling that begins to develop during this period is a child's feeling of competence. Either he gets the impression through his experience that he can get things done, or he begins to feel that he will outgrow his helplessness. This is a critical point in his development. What is your role as a parent in this process? The feeling of being effective should come about naturally as your child grows. When you think of it, the amount of progress that a child makes in language, in thinking, and in walking and running is quite remarkable in the early years. This should naturally add to his confidence. Your task then is to enhance and preserve this good feeling. You can best do this by supporting your child's efforts to acquire new skills. Overrestricting, criticizing, and even overassisting are actions which are likely to interfere with your child's developing a feeling of competence. Children at this age seem naturally to want to learn about things, yet they do have the problem that they may discourage easily.

We are plagued in this culture by the problem of competition. Everyone wants to be the best. This feeling often causes a child to abandon something he doesn't do well the first time he tries. In the long run, this works against him. Teaching, but even more important, showing an interest and getting involved, are ways you can give your child some specific help. This isn't easy. You have to learn how to back off if necessary and how to avoid showing impatience or disappointment when he is trying but doesn't get it easily. His enthusiasm is, to a large extent, a reflection of yours. A feeling of competence is a very important quality to develop as your child enters his elementary school years; once acquired, it tends to lead to success.

SUMMARY

This chapter has stressed the fact that although children are born with different physical, intellectual, and emotional qualities that make each one unique, they are all influenced by certain trends in development. If you are aware of these trends as a parent, you are in a better position to enhance your child's growth rather than interfere with it. You have a better acceptance of his refusal, his inability to share or to show sympathy at times, his need to touch things. We looked at some of the developmental characteristics of infants, toddlers, and preschool and kindergarten children. We noted that infants seem interested and capable of discovering things about the world around them from the time of birth. Young children need stimulation and support from you. They also need a certain degree of "space" to develop. They are limited to some extent by their stage of physical, neurological, and emotional development. They prefer concrete experience, and they learn a great deal from imitation. They are not always able to handle delay or other forms of frustration well, and they do not naturally take another person's point of view. On the other hand, they are very active learners who are generally filled with energy and enthusiasm. While you need to set limits and provide guidance, it is important that you support your child's vital growth needs when possible. It is important that these vital qualities be preserved by a supportive rather than a critical attitude from you.

ADDITIONAL READING

GESELLE, ARNOLD, et al., *The First Five Years of Life.* New York: Harper & Row, 1940.

HARLOW, HARRY, "The Nature of Love." *American Psychologist,* 13 (1958): 673–85.

MEAD, EUGENE D., *Six Approaches to Child Rearing.* Provo, Utah: Brigham Young University Press, 1976.

PIAGET, JEAN, AND INHELDER, B., *The Psychology of the Child.* New York: Basic Books, 1969.

chapter four
DISCOVERING YOURSELF AND YOUR OWN VALUES

Values underlie all of our behavior and attitudes whether we are aware of them or not. Certainly our ideas about how children should behave, what experiences they should have, and what goals we have for their future are based on our values. How aware are you of your own values? Are you aware in each case how they affect your interactions with your child, your expectations for her behavior, and your relationship with her generally? How do you identify your values? How do you determine the values that might be useful to try to encourage in your child?

Let's begin by taking a look at the relationship between your conscious and your unconscious values. The former are values that you profess. They may include avoiding prejudice, keeping your word, favoring women's rights, and supporting public education. Whatever they are, these values are the ones you are aware of. Unconscious values are ones that you may have not put into words but are implicit in what you do or say. For example, you may feel it necessary to win or place priority on material things even though you may not believe this to be true of you.

Sometimes your conscious and unconscious values are in conflict. This results in confusion for your child, especially if what you say and what you do are different. These basic conflicts of values are built into our culture. Consider our orientation toward children. We Americans regard ourselves as very child-oriented, yet we let children starve and spend less on health care and education than we do on entertainment and vacations. On a more personal level, we may work hard to provide our children with the basic necessities but may devote relatively little time talking to them, playing with them, and enjoying them. Then there are all of the things we tell children that we value that are not actually consistent with how we behave. We may tell them how important it is to tell the truth, for example, and then lie about their age in order to get them onto the train for half fare.

We say we value cooperation and sharing, yet we also emphasize competition in school, work, and play. We may say losing is fine as long as you play the game well, but our culture repeatedly reinforces the value "be a winner."

A materialistic orientation is another difficult value to overcome in our culture. We may tell our children to "stop asking for things," but we, along with them, are constantly bombarded by media advertising, particularly on TV, that incites us to buy the latest car, soap, stereo, etc., or feel like we are "out of it" or deprived.

Aggression is another area that provides a cultural source of conflict and is apt to be confusing for children, if not for parents. As we have become more aware of the value of expressing feelings, we have become more accepting as a culture of children's expressing their anger. While this is indeed desirable, it creates problems as children exercise a natural tendency to hit parents. We may also discourage hitting playmates, *"except when they hit you first."* These distinctions are difficult for young children to make. In those cases, they need to be aware of and remember who and under what conditions they may hit, if at all. They also have to learn to distinguish between expressing their anger verbally, which may be allowed, and expressing it physically, which may not. All of these distinctions may be complicated by the fact that in spite of what their parents may tell them, their parents may also hit them on occasion. More than once we have had a parent complain, "I don't understand why little Susie hits other children. I hit her every time she does it!"

Remember, children learn more from watching your behavior than they do from what you tell them. They tend to imitate your behavior and internalize your expressed values for themselves. That is why it is so important first to get in touch with your own feelings and values and then to consider the values you wish to impart to your child. As we noted in chapter 1, being aware of your own philosophy with respect to your child enables you to make more meaningful choices and to behave more consistently and with more conviction. It is useful to examine your interactions with your child and to notice where your actual behavior may be inconsistent with your stated values. This does not necessarily mean that you need to change how you are behaving. In some cases, your behavior may more truly reflect what you believe than your stated point of view. You may have been maintaining a particular value not out of personal conviction but because you believed it to be the socially acceptable position or because it had been what you were taught as a child. On the other hand, perhaps you would like to encourage a different value than your behavior has been suggesting to your child. In that case, it would be necessary to change your behavior to make it more consistent with the values you would like to promote.

Being aware of your values helps you to be more flexible as well as more consistent. You are not behaving automatically or resisting change simply on the basis of a traditional outlook. At the same time, you can use your value system to construct and reevaluate your plan for your child as well as a guideline for your interactions with your child. From a child's point of view, this makes you more reasonable. Literally, you have a reason for what you are doing. It's not "because I am your mother" or "because I say so." In addition, your statements and your actions are likely to be much more consistent when you are aware of your values and your goals. It is less confusing for a child when your values and your behavior are consistent, and this match will encourage her growth in a direction that you feel is worthwhile.

Once you have come to some decision about which values you wish to promote, you are faced with the difficult task of examining your own behavior to see how you are promoting those values. Let's take a few typical examples. How do you feel about manners? Have you thought about why they may be important to you? Is it just the formality or that it pleases you to see your child observe these traditions? Likely as not, you are at least as interested in promoting the values behind the manners: concern for and awareness of others. How do you deal with this? Do you require your child to say "please," "thank you," and "excuse me"? Or are you satisfied if she shows some awareness of others without going through the formal motions? In our preschool program we don't require formal behavior. We prefer that the children come to this stage more naturally as they observe our behavior toward them and toward the other children. We make a point of saying "thank you" and "please" to the children, which many times adults forget to do. We "model" the desired behavior and attitude. While the children don't always remember to say the words, we observe how their relationships with one another improve as the year continues.

Let's take another brief example from our school experience. Young children very often do not seem to notice or acknowledge each other's coming and going. Yet parents often insist that their children say "hello." Our experience has shown us that there is a better way to facilitate this awareness. Specifically, we have found that when we make a particular point of greeting each child as he or she enters the room and giving each a hearty "Goodbye, see you tomorrow" when leaving, the children not only feel good about it, but they also begin to say "hello" and "goodbye" to us and each other in a spontaneous way, imitating our action. It seems that the children are not just being mannerly, but they have a genuine interest and concern for one another.

In attempting to impart values, it is essential to keep your child's age in mind. A type of behavior that often creates problems for parents is what appears to be the "selfishness" of their young children. Actually this egocentricity is a natural characteristic of this developmental period. You may want your child to be considerate and share more, but your expectations must be age-appropriate. Children at two and three cannot really share. They can take turns. As a parent, you can model the desired interaction, and the child will begin to see how to act in a more considerate manner. For example, when one sibling pulls a toy from another, you can intervene by saying, "Joan is using it now. We'll use it when she has finished." Joan also needs to be reminded to tell when she's finished, and you have to be alert to follow through on the assurance. This intervention serves to reassure Sue and begins to teach Joan about the first step in sharing, which is taking turns.

Parents often forget to take their child's age into consideration when dealing with behavior in younger children that may be thought of as lying, cheating, or stealing in an older child. Very often preschool-age children are accused of these crimes by parents. Suppose a child takes some loose change that was left on the bedroom dresser. How would you react? You would probably want to let her know that you disapprove of such behavior and to warn her not to do it again, but it would not be appropriate or useful to treat her like a delinquent or to worry that if you don't shame her or punish her severely now, she will eventually be a delinquent. In fact, taking your change is a very typical type of experiment for a young child. It is similar with cheating. Young children generally do not play fair. They need to win. They usually try to make things turn out their way by changing rules, taking extra turns or extra pieces, etc. In the same way, they are likely to change the truth or deny what they have done. Again, this is a normal stage and need not be a cause for alarm or overreaction. On the other hand, you do not have to let it go unnoticed. In a game with you, you might let her win, but if she has denied doing something like taking money or hitting a younger brother, then you might remind her of what really took place and show your disapproval. You might also remind her of the importance of telling the truth. But keep in mind that the concept of truth or lying is too abstract a concept for a young child to really comprehend.

Intellectually, young children are not capable of understanding the concepts of reasoning that are involved in a fully developed value system. They also need time and experience to develop their own personalized value system, from their own observations, personal experiences, and intellectual growth.

Parents can assist by providing a model, the language, and supervision.

How do you know what is best for your child in terms of values that you have chosen to live your own life by as an adult? Unfortunately, there is no simple answer to this question. At a personal level, it is important to consider carefully the child's uniqueness as a person. In previous chapters we talked about individual differences. It is just as important to distinguish between you and your child in the area of values. You may share common values. But you each have different personalities and your own style of reactions and priorities. You may value friends and good company, for example. Your child may be a more solitary person even though she may share your concern for others in a larger sense.

In some areas you may feel so strongly that you can't allow for much variation. In the area of religion, for example, taking into account your child's young age, you may expect her to observe some of the rituals, hoping that someday she will be in a better position to understand the religious principles that these actions represent.

In other areas, you may choose to be somewhat more flexible, or you may not only take into account the world that you grew up in and the world today but also attempt to anticipate the cultural, political, social, and economic environment that is likely to exist for your child in the future.

What will the future be like? For some it is frightening to realize that the world that they are preparing their children for is apt to be very different from the society that exists today. But this does not mean that we have to be either resistant or helpless in the face of it. We can help our children to deal with an uncertain future by helping them to develop flexibility, open-mindedness, and creativity. We can help them to develop their ability to solve problems, think critically, make choices, and be self-directed.

Of course, uncertainty and change are only one aspect of the future, albeit a very significant one. But preparing your child for this and other future situations, such as increased technology, increased opportunities for women, and the diminished influence of traditions, requires a consideration of the values and the related skills you wish to encourage.

As we help our children to identify and reflect our values, we also get to know ourselves better. This brings us to a very important part of our chapter—how, in raising children, we are able to discover ourselves.

DISCOVERING YOURSELF

Parenthood can be a difficult task. One of the things that makes it difficult at times is that it puts some of your values to the test and requires you to make some significant changes in how you behave and how you feel. On the positive side, parenthood is an opportunity for you to learn more about yourself—an opportunity for self-discovery. You may have had a great many preconceptions about how you felt about children, how you might behave toward your own children, and what your expectations for them were. Faced with the actual experience of raising a particular child or children, you are likely to have to make some readjustments in what you do as well as in your attitudes and values. If you remain openminded, you will find that you are growing along with your child. This is apt to make you a better parent than if you were to hold fast to those preconceptions.

Let's take your attitude toward children in general. If you regarded yourself as a person who "loves children" and looked forward to parenthood, you might have gotten off to a good start, but not necessarily. You may have found that your infant was difficult to feed or that she slept very little. Perhaps this condition was brought on by colic, but it may have left you with a feeling of helplessness, guilt, anger, or disappointment. How could you, as a person who loves children, not be able to comfort your own baby; or how could you deal with the discovery that you resented how little time you now had for yourself?

If your infant was a delight at first, perhaps you found the experience of toddlerhood a horror, when she needed constant supervision as she rampaged through your house daily, seemingly trying to poison, maim, or electrocute herself when your attention was diverted to laundry, house cleaning, or cooking. In any event, perhaps you found that parenthood, while rewarding at times, was far less of a joy than you expected and that you even hated your child at times or regretted her presence. Does that make you a terrible person? Clearly not. This is a very human reaction. But it may affect your attitude toward children. That is, you may realize that they must be taken more seriously than dolls or other people's children you might have played with previously. You may decide that you don't really want to have fifteen kids of your own. Your attitude toward yourself may change, too. Instead of feeling guilty that you are not as able to love your child or children absolutely all of the time, you may become more realistic so that you are better able to accept them as imperfect and yourself as less than ideal, too. This is an extremely valuable form of self-discovery and growth for you.

Suppose you were never particularly enthusiastic about having children but did have a child either "accidentally" or because you were pressured by your spouse, parents, or friends. What happens now? You don't have to stick to your antikids attitude, even if child raising is at times just as unpleasant as you thought it would be. You may be able to discover the child within yourself that will find pleasure playing with your infant or toddler. Or you may take pride as a parent in your baby's first words, first steps, and the compliments she elicits from others. Even the questions, annoying at times, may be a delight at other times. It is good to try to get in touch with those feelings when you can. For example, if your baby daughter has just gotten hold of your lipstick and put it all over her face, certainly you may feel alarmed or annoyed, but if you are able to keep in mind what a delightful adventure she has just had and enjoy the ridiculous sight she must be, all painted up, you can be less severe and still communicate some constructive guidance.

Sometimes we forget to enjoy our children because we are all caught up with the responsibility. If you find the task of raising young children entirely burdensome, then you should really take a careful look at what is happening. Perhaps it is one of the two factors we've just suggested above; or a number of other things could be operating. You may feel a lack of support from your spouse. This is especially true for those women who have the primary responsibility for the care of their children. If you have had to give up or dramatically alter your career, it is tempting to direct your anger toward the child or subconsciously to be determined not to take pleasure in the experience of motherhood. Fathers also experience a change when young children are on the scene. You might resent the time your wife spends with the new baby and tend to be angry with the child for this. Obviously, it is helpful to get in touch with these feelings and, instead of taking them out on the child, to discuss them and attempt to work them out so you can enjoy your child. For the mother this may mean some relief from the daily pressure of child care or even finding an alternative child-care situation so you can return to work and spend constructive time with your child at other times during the day. For the father it may mean sharing responsibility for the baby's care or helping your wife to arrange her schedule so that you both have some time alone.

Many parents feel guilty when they take time away from their young child. But being a good parent requires a considerable expenditure of your emotional resources at times, and because of this it is often necessary, for your child as well as yourself, that you manage to spend time alone or on pursuits that are apart from her. The time away is potentially restorative for you and may consequently enable you to be more caring and effective when you are together with your child. Studies of working mothers, for example, reveal that if a mother is happy in her career she is able to be a more effective parent, while mothers who stay home but are discontent make less effective parents. If you are too preoccupied with your own problems or too overburdened with the daily responsibility of housekeeping and child care, you may need help from a family member or an outside agency such as a child guidance center. But the time you spend on your own is not necessarily bad for your child.

Let's look at it another way. In the long run, if you devote yourself to your role as a parent completely, you are not developing other aspects of your potential as a human being. We have learned that this sacrificing approach to motherhood makes you too dependent on your child to the point that you can't let her go when the time comes or that it leaves you with the feeling of a martyr. From the child's point of view, if you are working or have other interests, you are providing a favorable model of a person who is vital and interesting apart from her parenting role, which you may wish your child to emulate. You are also giving the child some space to develop her own style. This is an important part of the developmental process that many people never really completely accomplish. Psychologists use the term *individuation* to describe this process, whereby each person becomes someone in his or her own right, apart from parents, children, spouses, and others with whom one is closely identified. This process of individuation is important, but it is not always easy to effect. There are plenty of cultural prescriptions that make it especially difficult for a mother to abandon that role even temporarily, even if it may be in the best interest of her child as well as herself.

To accomplish your own individuation may require firmness and consistency. In some cases husbands as well as children may try to make you feel guilty about the time you take for yourself. Rather than succumbing to this pressure and resenting it or ignoring their concerns, take stock to see whether their complaints are at all legitimate and require modifications on your part. At the same time, keep the space for yourself that you may require.

In other cases you may find that it is you, as a parent, who has the difficult time separating yourself from your child. Here the same process applies. Take stock to see if there are areas where you can give your child more choice or more freedom. In a preschool child's case, you may need to see about putting a fence around your backyard so she can be outside on her own, or you may enroll her in a preschool program so she will have an opportunity to be in a social situation apart from you. You both will gain from learning that she is able to do quite well on her own.

Raising children also affords you the opportunity to discover your own hidden biases. For example, you may find that it is very difficult for you to deal with an active child, while your child's being constantly on the go does not seem to bother your spouse particularly. Or you may discover that the helplessness of your young infant is frightening to you and that you prefer your child at preschool age, while another parent prefers children when they are so "tiny." You may find that you rather enjoy your child's assertiveness, even though it gets in your way at times, or on the other hand, that you prefer your child to be generally compliant. To the extent that you become in touch with your personal biases as you interact with your child, you are in a position either to acknowledge and accept them or to reject and change them if you wish. This increased awareness is of personal benefit to you, and it is also useful in raising your child.

If you find your child is too clingy, you may need to "push her away" just to get some space of your own, only to find that the more you push, the more she seems to want to hang on. It is better for you to acknowledge this characteristic of yours, namely, that you do not like a clingy child. If you deny it by being very patient until you can't take it any longer, you are likely to blow up and demand that she get away from you. One solution might be to arrange for fairly regular brief separations by using a babysitter or child care program. The relief enables you to have more genuine patience for the times when you are together. In time, the child generally becomes less insecure about your relationship and less clingy when you are together.

You may discover that the worst episodes for your patience occur at a particular time, say at dinner time or in the early evening when she is going to bed and you need to be "off duty" for a while. If you are a parent who's been at home most of the day, that may be a good time to get your spouse involved. It is helpful to avoid doing this as a last resort, when you are frantic. It is most alarming if you shove your child at your spouse, shouting, "Take her, she's yours. I can't stand her any more." However, if the other parent takes over the evening routine on a preplanned basis, it is usually a good experience for everyone involved.

You also might take a look at how you relate to certain materials and activities that being a parent is likely to expose you to. How important is neatness to you, for example? Do you allow your child to make a mess or do you allow yourself to get dirty? At times you really need to let your child play with household items if they are safe, to play with water, under supervision, or to paint. By resisting these activities or staying aloof from them yourself, you are not only revealing your prejudice but you are also signaling to your child that there is something wrong with the activity, the material, or even the child herself for liking it.

In this same area, child rearing gives you a chance to test out your attitude toward sex-role stereotyping. As we will point out later, our tendency to limit our sons and daughters because of their sex is very insidious. How do you react when your son asks for a doll of his own or when your daughter says "Only boys are doctors" as she selects a nurse's kit in the toy store?

To the extent that your reactions to your child's behavior help you to learn about your own values and attitudes, you can learn a great deal about yourself in the child-rearing process. In that regard, if you are openminded, you are likely to find that you are growing along with your child. Don't be surprised, however, if your child seems very rigid and stubborn at times, even if you attempt to present her with a different model. In the long run, if you are open and reasonable while still firm about guidelines and the values that these represent, you are likely to find that your child will eventually be able to be more flexible and reasonable herself. If you have a fairly good understanding of your own values and preferences, you can be more assured as you set necessary limits and standards for your child. As her understanding skills mature, she will be better able to see your guidelines as less arbitrary and more reasonable than they may appear to be in preschool years.

ADDITIONAL READING

SIMON, SIDNEY B.; HOWE, LELAND W.; AND KIRSCHENBAUM, HOWARD, *Values Clarification*. New York: Hart, 1972.
SIMON, SIDNEY B., AND WENDUS, SALLY, *Helping Your Child Learn Right from Wrong: A Guide to Values Clarification*. New York: Simon & Schuster, 1976.

chapter five
ASPECTS
OF DISCIPLINE

What do you mean when you use the term discipline? For some parents, discipline is a means of fitting children into a mold that has been precast by society or by their own expectations of what a "good child" and ultimately what a "good adult" might be like. For other parents, discipline refers to the notion of guidelines and restraints, or what are sometimes called "limits." Rather than directing the child's behavior, it suggests helping them to give some shape and purpose to their own needs and actions.

The term *discipline* is sometimes thought of as being synonymous with spanking or physical punishment. Even though the terms are sometimes used interchangeably, discipline is not the same as punishment. In *Schools without Failure,* William Glasser distinguished between discipline and punishment as follows:

> In punishment, pain follows an act that someone else disapproves of, and the someone else usually provides the pain; with discipline, in contrast, the pain is a natural and realistic consequence of a person's behavior.*

*William Glasser, *Schools without Failure* (New York: Harper and Row, Pub., 1969), p. 27.

Discipline enables the child to avoid negative consequences or, if not, to change her behavior to produce a more favorable outcome.

In our own view, discipline is a constructive form of guidance. It is not punishment for punishment's sake or a "breaking of the will." It is limits and structuring situations for a child with the goal of developing her ability to control her own actions. In this way, control gradually shifts from adults to the child.

This shift of control is not a sudden process, nor can it be accomplished completely in the early years. Preschool children have not yet reached the stage of conscience development, nor can they easily take another person's perspective. They usually comply not because of some inner sense of right and wrong but because of external controls and reminders that you provide. Gradually they should be helped to manage on their own without always relying on your reminders and controls. Your consistent and constructive guidance will help them to develop these inner controls.

DISCIPLINE DEVELOPS CONTROLS

There is a great deal of individual variation in a child's personality and behavior from the time of birth (many would say before birth). Some infants seem to resist direction from the outside, while others passively comply with external demands, showing no signs of distress. Most, of course, show a little of both. In fact, you can learn a lot about your baby by noticing in which areas she seems to require more independence. You can also make provision for this need when possible, and, among other benefits, you will probably have fewer discipline problems. For example, your toddler may prefer walking around without benefit of your helping her balance even though it is difficult for you to resist offering your hand. You may have discovered your child attempting to feed herself long before she seemed really capable. It is important to encourage this early independence even though quite a mess might result. While all children are not as vigorous or as early in seeking independence, this is an inevitable aspect of growing up that is likely to emerge at several points in the preschool years even if it is not a consistent feature of your child's personality.

There are some specific times in development that we have already discussed where a child generally shows a desire to "do it myself" or to say "no" a lot. This, we have learned, is generally a sign of healthy resistance to parental control, although admittedly it can be a problem for you when it emerges, especially if your child had always been a nice, cooperative kid before she made her bid for power. You may be tempted to put such a child in her place. You may just be worried that if this trend keeps up, you will have a juvenile delinquent on your hands. It is indeed important to set limits in these situations, for your own sake as well as the child's. On the other hand, keep in mind that young children also need to feel that they can be effective. They also need to experience a sense of control over their own actions and even a sense of power at times, within limits. It is important that, as a parent, you allow adequate space for that growth and that you enlarge that space appropriately as your child develops.

Achieving a balance between a child's need for autonomy and your responsibility to provide a framework for growth is not an easy task. For example, Freud talked about the significance of the struggle between the child and her parents in the process of toilet training. The child, after all, is being asked to control a natural function. Freud pointed out that *how* this process is accomplished is as important as *whether* it is accomplished. He argued against toilet training at any cost because he discovered that the feelings associated with this experience were apt to survive well beyond childhood.

The same principle applies to all aspects of asking your child to comply with your standards. If the child feels that she has capitulated to parental demands because she had no choice (after all, parents are bigger and stronger than children), then she is likely to feel defeated. On the other hand, when she is ready and able to comply out of her own free will, she is likely to feel triumphant rather than compromised.

CHILDREN NEED GUIDELINES

There was a time when professionals advocated what has been termed a "permissive" approach to child rearing. This was a reaction against the repressive authoritarian techniques that had been used earlier. This point of view suggested that discipline in any form was really unnecessary and that a child raised in a benevolent environment would inevitably chart her own course in a direction that was best suited to her. A. S. Neil, a well-known British educator, founded a school based on the idea that children should be completely free to make their own choices about what they wanted to learn and how they want to live. The title of his best-selling book, *Summerhill,* has become synonymous with a permissive education.

Most professionals recognize that children need more boundaries than Neil advocated. Restrictions are a necessary part of guidance and are actually more liberating to a child than no boundaries at all. A good illustration of this point is giving choices to your preschool child. For example, if you offer your child an unlimited choice of what to eat or what to wear, she is less likely to be able to make a specific final choice than if you were to give her two options ("the yellow one or the red one"). In the latter case, she is likely to come away from the experience feeling good for having made a decision for herself, and you will have avoided considerable wear and tear on your nerves.

BASICS OF DISCIPLINE

Keeping your goals for child rearing in mind, think to yourself, "What am I trying to accomplish?" as you practice techniques of discipline. For example, if your goal is to help your child to develop a sense of cooperation, it is inappropriate to punish your child for not sharing her favorite toy. Even though she *may* comply with your wishes the next time, she isn't likely to develop a good feeling about sharing. It would be preferable to take a more positive action, such as encouraging her to share after she's had some time ("Andrea will play with it for a few minutes, and when she is done she'll tell me and we'll give it to you.") By the same token, if your goal is to teach her that hitting is not acceptable, hitting her for hitting another child is also inappropriate. When discipline is not effective, very often it is because you have lost sight of your original goal. Your anger or hurt pride begins to direct your actions as this takes place. Parents frequently remark, "I know that this punishment isn't working, but it makes *me* feel better." It is best to stop short of this situation. If your approach to discipline isn't working, step back a bit and analyze the situation to see if you can discover why not. Perhaps you need to change your strategy to reach your goal.

SOME GOALS FOR DISCIPLINE

You may have many particular goals for a specific discipline situation. We like to keep in mind four basic goals that we consider to be fundamental to the process of discipline:

1. that the child not hurt herself or others
2. that the child behave according to some socially acceptable standard
3. that the child ultimately be able to control and direct her own actions
4. that the child feel good about herself in the process; that is, she must have a feeling of satisfaction, accomplishment, and even autonomy while she is learning the give-and-take of cooperative living.

DISCIPLINE SHOULD BE REASONABLE

You should have a worthwhile reason for limiting or punishing your child. Discipline involves designing limits and rules that are consistent with your values, your child's developmental needs, and the promotion of cooperative living in your household. As often as possible, children should have a part in developing the rules. Whenever possible, you should share the reason for limits with your child, offering a brief and simple explanation if conditions permit. In this way you demonstrate that your actions are not arbitrary, even if your child is unable to accept them at first. Eventually, your explanation will become meaningful to your child. A simple example is wearing a hat in cold weather. Many young children don't like the restriction of a hat and will resist putting one on. It is important that your child wear, it like it or not, if you feel that it is necessary because of the possibility of an ear infection or a cold. You may simply insist—your will against hers—but it is helpful if you remind her that she only has to wear it on cold days, so she won't get sick, and that she can take it off as soon as she gets inside. This brief explanation tempers the restriction somewhat, while it gives the child a context in which to place the temporary discomfort. In the long run, the child will begin to see the connection between the cold weather and the need for wearing a hat where otherwise she is only preoccupied with your infringement on her freedom.

DISCIPLINE AS A CONSEQUENCE OF EXPERIENCE

Obviously, you can't let your child burn herself to show her the negative consequences of touching a flame or a hot stove, but you can allow her to miss dessert if she hasn't eaten her dinner or not to play outside if she hasn't helped to pick up the toys in her room. These types of disciplinary actions can be presented as an extension of the behavior of which you disapprove: "Since you are too full for dinner, you must not have room for dessert" or "I had to use all the time cleaning your room without your help, so there will be no time left to play outside." Some behaviors, such as putting your hand on a hot stove, lead to a natural consequence. In that case, the child achieves a sense of self-control or discipline simply by learning that she can avoid getting a potentially painful burn by resisting the impulse to touch the stove. Eventually, she will be able to discriminate between situations when a stove may be cold and when it is hot and therefore painful to touch.

Much of what a child needs to learn consists of that kind of discrimination. Which objects in her home can she play with and which ones should she avoid? She may need you to help her to learn these discriminations. "I can't let you play with the little glass animals in the living room because they may break, but you may play with the plastic ones that I bought for you." If this is not effective, a second step is to inform the child of the consequences of her behavior: "If you do not put away your plastic toys after the bath, you will have to bathe without them next time."

Allowing children to experience the consequences of their own behavior or even reminding them of the consequences, as we've described, doesn't imply that they fully understand cause and effect. They are only beginning to explore this concept intellectually at the early childhood level, but even before they acquire a fuller understanding of cause and effect, they intuitively respond to the consequences of their acts if these consequences are consistent and they occur reasonably close to the time of their behavior.

Another example of this is when a young child spills milk or juice. You may be tempted to yell or punish, but a more effective technique if you can keep your cool (which is not always possible) is to note the effect ("Oh, your milk spilled"), provide reassurance if necessary ("That's OK"), and offer a solution ("Here is a sponge you can use to clean it up"). This is more constructive and usually less likely to escalate the problem than either punishment or scolding. You know from your own experience that if you are tense about spilling, forgetting a person's name, etc., that tension is likely to contribute to the dreaded event's occurring.

APPROACHES AND TECHNIQUES OF DISCIPLINE

Keeping your goals and development in mind, there are a variety of approaches and techniques of discipline you might adopt. In this chapter we've included several for your consideration, while noting the ones we favor as being consistent with the goal of parents and children growing together.

The Authoritarian Approach

The authoritarian approach to discipline assumes that the parent is the ultimate and sole source of power in the relationship between parent and child. This point of view may be verbalized to an older child when he is told, in effect, "As long as you are living under my roof, you will do as I say!" With younger children, this attitude may take a more benevolent tone, at least at first. An infant is a pretty helpless creature, and many parents particularly enjoy this stage because the baby is so dependent and accepts help. But you may encounter resistance, even during the early stages of a child's life. Initially it may come in the form of a resistance to eating or to sleeping. Then, as we've noted, the drive for independence and the ability to assert herself is likely to get stronger as she begins to toddle around. Speech accelerates the process. Soon she can say "no" in a defiant way and eventually can begin to question your direction and to argue. Your attitude as a parent may still be essentially a benevolent one. You may wish to protect your child from danger or just to have her behave in a way which is socially acceptable. It is tempting under these circumstances to rely on your position as the authority: "You do it because I said so." We have found several problems with this approach.

Children who are raised in an authoritarian style may appear to be misleadingly well behaved at first glance, but frequently they are quite rebellious when not supervised. In addition, even though you want your child to behave properly, you need to ask, on what basis? Your child may be complying with your wishes out of fear or even because she loves you (actually, fear is involved here, too, because she is afraid of losing your love). But, if you believe that a child should develop internal controls—that is, that she behave not just because she is afraid but because she has some understanding and acceptance of your point of view— then an authoritarian approach to discipline is not a good choice for you.

Children cannot be allowed to hurt other people or to destroy property. They are not in a position to handle unlimited choice. Their behavior is affected by and affects other people.

When and where they eat, whether or not they go to school, to bed, etc., is not simply determined by their own desires. Parents do have the responsibility for determining the outside limits for these behaviors. But within these limits, a child's point of view, even that of a very young child, can be taken into account. A very obvious example is feeding an infant. Even though the infant is preverbal, he can communicate to you whether he is hungry or not. This choice of when to eat may not always fit your schedule, but the degree to which you can compromise with the infant as to how often and when it's time to eat, you are respecting your child's individuality and allowing her to participate in decision making, even at this very young age.

Even professionals sometimes have problems in this regard. A colleague who is a pediatric nurse had been told by the obstetrician in charge of her ward not to feed the newborn babies until twenty-four hours after birth. She noticed that for some infants this was not a major problem, but for others it proved to be very upsetting. They seemed to be born hungry. If she withheld food for twenty-four hours as she had been instructed, the hungry infants showed signs of distress throughout that period. On the other hand, if she gave them a meal, they were able to quiet down and get some rest. What do you think she chose to do?

On a broader societal level, times have changed with regard to society's blanket acceptance of authority. It is no longer necessarily the sign of a good citizen to comply passively with laws that may be unjust. The civil rights movement, the women's rights movement, and the Viet Nam war have taught us that. We even question the actions of the head of state, the President, Watergate being the prime example. The children we are raising are the citizens of the future and must be ready to question abuses of power. Young children are not yet capable of making critical judgments, but a two-way communication process between you and your child expands that possibility.

Another politically related change in parent-child relationships is the fact that children are no longer considered to be the exclusive property of their parents. Children are protected by law against neglect and abuse, against having to work at an early age, and against being denied an education. As your child matures, she is likely to be encouraged to express her feelings and ideas and to take part in decision making. A child who is dominated by authority will be unable to do so.

The Authoritative Approach

The authoritative approach to discipline differs from the authoritarian approach in that the parent does not control the child by force or by a superior position. The authoritative parent attempts to tune in to the child's needs and style of doing things, while still retaining control of the situation. As we've noted, even an infant's individuality can be respected. Once the child is old enough, she may be allowed to question and to participate in setting rules and limits. Yet the parent remains in charge, in that the freedom increasingly offered the child has its boundaries. Parents guide the child toward self-control by expanding opportunities for independence as she matures. This does not mean you allow a child to do whatever she wants or allow her to badger you into granting a privilege.

It is not easy to be an authoritative parent. It may be tempting to resort to the rule of force or, on the other hand, to bow to pressure to please the child. It is important to keep in mind that the parent who gives a child freedom without responsibility is not doing that child a favor. The child who is truly free needs to be able to control herself. Children who have been given freedom without preparation are usually victims of their own impulses, while too much discipline of the authoritarian kind also leaves children helpless because they are either too dependent on direction or they are always resisting it. Optimally, children would be guided to the point where they are able to make responsible decisions for themselves. These responsible decision makers are in touch with their own needs and feelings, but they are also aware of the needs and feelings of others. They do not need to defy others in order to prove themselves.

The key to a successful authoritative approach to discipline—or, for that matter, to any successful interpersonal relationship—is a process in which all concerned have a contribution to make, and the resulting decision or behavior is a product of a give-and-take on everyone's part. This "interactive style" suggests that, in the parent-child relationship, communication goes two ways, from parents to child and from child to parents.

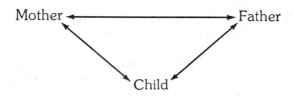

This does not mean that child and parent are on an equal basis, nor does it mean that a child necessarily gets her way. It suggests that there is a mutuality between parents and child, a two-way process whereby parents and children really hear one another, as opposed to the situation where they are protesting their own points of view. It means that if a child cannot do something at one point, for example, her expression of disappointment will be accepted by her parents and, if possible, provision may be made for her being able to do what she wants at another point. When you are dealing with a young child, you need to take into account that she may find it more difficult than an adult to put off something she wants to do until later, or more difficult to see another person's point of view. But she will learn from experience that you are faithful to your word and that you are concerned about how she feels. Realizing this may not eliminate her whole disappointment, but it will go a long way toward making the limits and controls more bearable.

"Love-oriented" Techniques

Some parents control children through the generation of guilt. You may tell your child how disappointed you are in her behavior or how she has "let you down." Young children frequently do not respond directly to these types of statements because they really don't feel sorry in the sense that we might as adults. Mostly they feel afraid. Afraid of what, since you may not have threatened to punish them? They are afraid of losing your love and protection.

They may say they are sorry on that basis or offer to help to clean up a spill or make restitution. They eventually feel guilty or ashamed as they begin to internalize your standards, but usually this doesn't happen until age seven or older. Mostly they are afraid. This technique does work. Guilt has an advantage over force as a technique of control because it works in your absence. The child who is simply afraid of punishment might do something when you are not looking and hope not to get caught. But a child who is afraid of losing your love is controlled by a feeling of guilt even when you are not around to see what she has done.

"Love-oriented" techniques are the favorite form of discipline for middle-class parents (as opposed to power-oriented techniques). The problem with this approach in the long run is that if it is used too extensively, it can be overly effective in that the child grows up with a great burden of guilt that arises from the inevitable failure to live up to your standards. Of course, if you keep your standards reasonable and don't tell the child how disappointed you are too often, you may find it desirable that your child feel appropriately guilty when she has done something of which you don't approve.

Behavioral Techniques

Behavioral psychology has taught us about the importance of accepting small gains. Too often, as parents, we are disappointed when our child falls short of a desired goal in dinner-table behavior, toilet training, etc. We may feel like a failure ourselves every time the child has an accident or in other ways doesn't maintain a "perfect score." Learning theory has demonstrated that if we praise the child's success, however small it may be, and try to ignore or minimize the failures, the successes will grow in frequency. When you are disappointed and get discouraged, chances are your child feels the same way. Once you both give up hope or emphasize the failures, it is not likely that she will be able to move forward. Failure can become a habit just as easily as success.

Behavioral techniques emphasize controlling the environment to produce desirable behavior. In humanistic terms, this means anticipating, whenever possible, those situations where your child is apt to misbehave so that you can change the conditions to make misbehavior less likely. We have already given examples of preparing for a long car ride or waiting in line. Another example is taking your child into a home where there are lots of small breakable objects around that are tempting to touch. The child very likely will want to touch things, and in turn you will need to say no. This cannot be entirely avoided, but if you remember to take along some of your child's own playthings, then you can establish an area where she can be busy and therefore less likely to want to play with the forbidden objects. Another solution to this problem is to visit in a part of the house, the kitchen perhaps, that features fewer "no's."

Some behavioral techniques, although not always consistent with a humanistic orientation, are often effective short-range tools you may wish to employ in setting limits for your child. An increasingly popular and quite helpful technique is "time out." This helps to break the cycle of arguing with your child and in that respect works well with stubborn children. Time out works like this: if your child persists in doing something which is annoying you or of which you disapprove, let her know that if she doesn't stop (that is a warning), she will have to take a "time out." A "time out" is a brief period (as little as three minutes works for young children) when the child goes (willingly or not to her room and stays there until time is up. You may want to use a kitchen timer to remind you and your child when it is OK to come out of the room. The child is treated positively at that point unless she continues the unacceptable behavior, in which case she has to return for another three-minute period. This approach spares the elaborate explanations and offers a preschool child a simple, concrete way to replace her unacceptable behavior with something more desirable. This is particularly useful for dealing with disruptive behavior.

Spanking

How about spanking? Let us assume that you are against violence and have no intention of beating your child. Is hitting ever acceptable? Ultimately, this is a decision that you must make for yourself, in cooperation with your spouse. We, like most professionals, are opposed to spanking. Spanking is similar to punishment; it is not constructive. Although it may suppress unacceptable behavior, it doesn't teach positive alternatives. Another major concern with spanking is that it will get out of hand. In fact, many children are hurt by parents who are punishing in this way. On the other hand, some parents find that a single hand slap is useful when a young child has repeatedly touched something dangerous or highly breakable. For other parents, a single swat on the rear is effective when used *sparingly* to express serious disapproval. The act tends to be more symbolic and registers as a concrete and immediate signal for the child to stop. If you do choose to do this, it is important to be vigilant about not escalating this type of reprimand and not to use it too often. You should also note the effect on the child. Some children respond quickly, but for others it seems to cause even further resistance. In the latter case, it is best to select another technique.

Our humanistic orientation makes it difficult for us to accept hitting even in its most controlled form, although we realize that under some circumstances there may be no alternative.

INTERPERSONAL TECHNIQUES

Practice What You Preach

As we've said, children learn from observing, certainly as much as from what they are told. If you are not in the habit of putting away your things after you have used them, don't expect that your child will do any better. Remember the old expression, "actions speak louder than words."

Keep Rules at a Minimum

Young children aren't able to keep in mind a great many rules. If you have lots of rules, then they will need lots of reminders, which isn't good for either you or the child. You know how terrible you feel if all you ever hear yourself saying is "no" or "I told you not to do that." Whether you know it or not, it is equally as unpleasant for the child. Too many rules also are apt to give a child the feeling of being restricted.

Avoid Nagging

Reminders are helpful, but if they are too frequent and too persistent, they have a tendency to backfire. Children who are nagged (for that matter, husbands or wives, too) are not apt to comply. They either turn you off or actually do the opposite. If you find yourself nagging, then you probably need to change your approach.

Back Off When Necessary

Sometimes, when you are locked into a struggle with your child, it is useful to back off a bit. When you detach yourself from the immediate situation, you give yourself some time to cool off and you also gain some perspective on the situation. A good technique here is to pretend that you are dealing with someone else's child. You are almost always calmer and more reasonable.

FACTORS THAT INTERFERE WITH EFFECTIVE DISCIPLINE

Discipline seems to be a major problem for many parents. By examining those factors that generally interfere with effective discipline, you can see how these might relate to your own experience.

The Child Within Us

One reason that discipline is difficult for parents is that they identify with their children. They are committed to making up for the unpleasantness they experienced in their own childhood. They may also be taking the part of the child who is being punished or restricted. That is why sometimes parents cannot work well together in disciplining their child. One parent sends the child to her room and the other sneaks up with a sandwich or a word of comfort. This conflict even takes place with a single parent who may deny a privilege, TV, for example, and later feels so bad for the child who is missing her favorite show that she calls the child in to watch. To some extent, it is certainly a good thing that as a parent you also remember what it was like to be a child, but if you identify too strongly with the child in this way, your pain at the child's suffering prevents you from following through on discipline when it is appropriate. Saying no on occasion is a requirement of responsible parenting.

Wanting Your Child to Like You

Another thing that might get in the way of your being an effective parent is a desire to be popular with your child. It is indeed devastating when your child says, "I hate you!" Modern parents seem to be especially caught up with the need to be liked by their children. (Perhaps parents in earlier times didn't have this problem because they didn't allow their children to say how they felt when they were angry at them?)

To be a responsible parent, one has to accept the fact that your child will resent restrictions and is apt to get angry at you for imposing them.

Not Wanting to Crush Your Child

Another problem for parents is balancing their desire not to crush their children with their need to direct or discipline them at times. Most parents would like to see their children be able to develop their maximum potential as individuals. Perhaps they have had the experience themselves of always feeling obligated to do what others expected them to do or of not being able to assert their own individuality when necessary. They may want their children to have more choice and to be less concerned with following other directions than they might have been. Such parents may be reluctant to discipline their children. Some parents actually maintain that they do not wish unduly to influence their children's development. While the goal of personal development is a commendable one, it is easy to see how this misguided "hands-off" policy can get out of hand. If fact, if it is practiced too diligently, it can have an opposite effect than the one desired.

Young children require direction and guidance. They do not come into this world fully capable of making wise choices for themselves. They can eventually discover a great deal for themselves, but they need the help of parents and other adults in observing, problem solving, and decision making. They also must learn the sociopolitical context in which they are living and how to adjust to its realities as well as to the realities of the physical world. You are just as likely to "crush" your child by allowing her to negotiate this growth path without your assistance, as you would be doing all the work for her.

Changing Standards

Standards of behavior are less clear than they were when we were children. In these fast-paced, rapidly changing times, what had been true about children's manners, dress, relationship to adults, and just about every other aspect of sociocultural development is open to examination. Standards are no longer fixed by religion, society, culture, and family tradition. Parents are often required to set their own standards for children rather than rely on the ready-made ones. This problem is further complicated by the fact that children and parents are likely to encounter many different points of view in the neighborhood, in school, on TV, and in newspapers and magazines.

Standards are not only less clear than they were previously, but they are also less uniform. Parents are confronted with the fact that other children may have a different set of standards than their children. This puts parents in a vulnerable position. They are told more than ever that Johnny or Jane's parents are kinder and less strict than they are. Again, the pressure to abandon discipline and to allow what other parents do may be very tempting, so it is important for parents to have standards.

These standards don't have to be carved in stone. That is, they may be reasonable and flexible, but standards to which the child can refer nonetheless.

Your Ways vs. Your Parents'

Contemporary parents cannot always fall back on child-rearing practice that their own parents used. It would be simpler and easier if we could rely on the old methods, but while many of those ideas were appropriate for their time, they do require reexamination. For example, parents used to place much greater emphasis on behavior than on feelings. You might not have been able to tell your parents you were angry with them. Or you might have been told "It's nothing" when you fell or cried because you had to share a toy. Boys were discouraged from crying and girls were not expected to display anger. We are now aware that these practices forced us to submerge feelings or to behave in gender-stereotypical ways, but they were the standard way in which children were raised at the time. On that basis, you may wish to change your approach to parenting, but you may find that this is difficult sometimes and that in spite of your best intentions, you resort to techniques which you experienced as a child. This isn't so bad unless you would like to do something different. How often have you reminded yourself of your own parents in dealing with your children when you were determined not to?

SUMMARY

We have offered you some thoughts and some guiding principles regarding discipline here. As we've pointed out earlier, a young child is not able to appreciate another person's point of view or to reason as an adult would. Consequently, it is a gradual transition from the outside direction of parents to the child's development of her own inner controls, a shift from the child's compliance out of a fear of getting caught to compliance based on mutual understanding and concern for others. In order to accomplish this transition from outer to inner control, children need a good model of someone who cares about others, especially them, which you may provide. They also need to know why limits are being set. A brief explanation that they can understand about the rule or principle applied makes discipline more meaningful, more effective, and less frustrating.

You have to work out your own point of view and your own style in this very difficult but very important aspect of child rearing. Likely as not, you will not always be able to behave as rationally as you would like in the "heat" of the situation.

Parents are people too. As Thomas Gordon points out in *Parent Effectiveness Training,* you may not always be able to keep your cool. Any parent who has been cooped up with two or three young children (or even one for that matter) who have colds for a few days in winter can appreciate how difficult it can be to be rational at times. At other times your child might catch you off guard or hit a sensitive spot (we all have our "pet peeves").

Your children need to learn about you, too. Young children aren't able to empathize fully, but they can begin to read the signals. We all have a threshold that varies with the situation and our particular sensitivities. If you lose your balance for the moment, it is always possible to restore it, even if it means an apology from you or a change of strategy. A technique that we have both used with our own children when we are backed into a corner or we are beginning to lose control is to consider what we would do in the same situation if the child was someone else's, not ours. This puts a little distance between our charged-up emotions and provides an objectivity to the situation that allows for a more rational strategy. Always keep in mind that it is not worth sacrificing your relationship with your child to protect your own pride. Keep in mind that the most essential ingredient in this process is your overall concern and love for your child.

ADDITIONAL READING

GINOTT, HAIM, *Between Parent and Child.* New York: Macmillan, 1965.

GLASSER, WILLIAM, *Schools without Failure.* New York: Harper and Row, Pub., 1969.

NEIL, A. S., *Summerhill: A Radical Approach to Childrearing.* New York: Hart and Company, 1960.

THOMAS, GORDON, *Parent Effectiveness Training.* New York: Wyden, 1970.

chapter six
COMMUNICATING WITH YOUR CHILD

Communication is a popular term these days. It is a name for an industry as well as a field of study in college. When applied specifically to the exchange between two people, it is sometimes called "interpersonal communication." It is in this sense that we are using the term here: a reciprocal interaction between you and your child during which each party delivers a message that very likely influences the other. Some of these messages and their influences are subtle, while others are more obvious. Nevertheless, they are all part of an ongoing communication process that exists between parent and child.

What kinds of messages are being exchanged? Some of the messages are factual, like "That is a dog" or "Green means go." Some are cultural, like "Please wash your hands before dinner" or "Say 'thank you' to Grandma when she brings you a gift." Some messages are more specifically attitudinal, like "Nice little boys don't do that" or "Schoolwork comes first." Then there are the more indirect messages you deliver by selecting which of your child's behaviors you praise, such as "Nice catch, Willie" or "My, you look pretty, Susan." Very often the tone of your voice communicates a message which may or may not agree with the words you are saying. How many times have you said "That's all right, Honey," when your voice conveyed "I'm really upset by what you did"?

Throughout the process of communicating with your child you are imparting values. You are telling him, in words or otherwise, what you think is important (your priorities) and what is acceptable. Perhaps the most important message you communicate to your child is what you think of him. His view of himself is largely a reflection of how you see him. You let him know if he is good or bad, lovable or unlovable, competent or incompetent, and so on. On the other hand, what has he communicated to you? He has let you know by his behavior as well as through his words whether or not he regards you as a good parent. He has let you know whether or not he likes you. He has also let you know his interests, his personality, and what he thinks of himself, if you are sensitive to the messages. Take a moment and think about the messages you and your child have been delivering to one another. Have you been able to help him feel good about himself? How does he perceive you? How do you perceive him?

DEVELOPMENTAL ASPECTS
OF COMMUNICATION

Infants

There has been an increasing amount of research done of late on the communication between infants and their caretakers. After getting beyond the initial phase of studying the effects of mothers on children, psychologists, most notably Richard Bell of the National Institute of Mental Health, noted that babies have an effect on their mothers as well. Infants that take food well and are generally easy to care for are generally responded to more favorably by their mothers, and infants who are also prone to smile easily, are low in irritability, and like to cuddle are especially likely to receive lots of positive attention from their mothers in terms of talking, holding, and stroking. More recently, Bell and his associates have been studying the "reciprocity" between babies and mothers. They observed that the process goes back and forth; baby reinforces mother, mother, in turn, is more responsive to baby, and so on.

In speaking to your baby you are giving him the experience of hearing speech, which he will later imitate. If he hears lots of positive language, he is more likely to want to talk and to communicate. It has a positive meaning for him. It also gives him a favorable orientation about social interaction generally and a favorable attitude toward others, which is likely to get him positive feedback from others in return. This is how "social reciprocity" works.

When you are talking to your infant or young baby, it is important that you speak to him in a normal manner. But even more important than your words at this point especially, as we've said, is your tone of voice. It is a good idea to try to become aware of how you sound when you speak to your child, regardless of his age; but remember, an infant is not able to understand your words, so he is very dependent on the tone of voice for meaning. Sometimes we lose sight of the fact that we may sound mostly impatient, annoyed, or even much like a military field marshal when talking to our children. Do a bit more repeating with an infant and keep your language less wordy, using short sentences. Most important is the feeling you convey. It is helpful if your language isn't too businesslike; in other words, it should have an affectionate, friendly tone. That is the most significant message being delivered, especially before your infant is able to understand the meaning of your words.

Toddlers

Toddlers are beginning to understand the symbolic nature of language—that is, that words stand for things. They are attaching experience to words. It gives them a good feeling as they begin to label and identify. It also gives you, as a parent, an opportunity to teach your child certain expressions such as "hot," "no," "thirsty?" that are beginning to have meaning for him. He is able to identify his needs, and this is, of course, very useful. It certainly takes the guesswork out somewhat and makes life less frustrating for you as well as for your child.

Children learn language through imitation. If you keep your language relatively simple and clear, you are more likely to be understood and imitated. On the other hand, you don't have to sound like Tarzan of the Apes, speaking in one word sentences. It's a matter of simplifying your language somewhat so that you still offer your child a linguistic context which he can begin to appreciate and later imitate when his own language becomes more elaborate. Keep in mind here again what is important. Try to offer your child a pleasant and civilized tone where possible, although when you are displeased your tone and your words should reflect it. In that regard, at this time in your child's life, but at all stages really, try to avoid extremes. All of us have overheard parents threatening children with bodily harm or with abandonment or otherwise saying devastating things about a child's character ("You rotten kid") or competence ("You can't do anything right"); these statements may not be meant literally, but they are very apt to be taken that way.

This brings us to a related point. Children at this age are especially literal. If you say, "I'll do it in a minute," they expect it to happen quickly. Or if you say, "I'm going to tell that policeman to lock you up," the child may not fully understand but expects it literally to happen.

Toddlers test, as we've said. They need to know that exploration, curiosity, and even refusal are acceptable under particular circumstances, even though they may not be acceptable at a time that you specify. This is a difficult distinction to communicate. You might try to point it out even as you are setting a limit. For example, if you don't want your toddler to play with valuable and breakable porcelain items on your coffee table, you can provide him with some unbreakable animal figures or small cars of his own that he may play with on the floor or a table instead of the things he must learn not to touch. You are helping him to learn to distinguish between those things he may play with and those he should not. He may not accept the alternative easily, but you are likely to be more successful with a preschool child than a toddler, and it seems preferable to just saying no to the child without offering any constructive alternative.

Preschoolers

Preschool children are able to give you more of an idea of how they have perceived what you've told them. Of course, their language and understanding is still limited, even though they may have an impressive vocabulary. In many respects young children are quite candid. They say what is on their minds and report what they see. You may well be embarrassed as your preschooler says out loud, "Mommy, look at that fat lady." It is good to try to teach him what things he'd better whisper, because he might hurt someone's feelings, but remember that he is just telling what he sees and trying out new words and concepts—you don't want to discourage that. You might also find that as your preschool child begins to develop his language skills, he may be reluctant to show them off on your cue. You may want him to tell you something about an experience, or to tell grandmother something cute he had said previously, and he refuses. This is likely to be disappointing to you, but keep in mind that this is developmentally appropriate. His resistance is a form of control. He doesn't always feel like performing "on command." Spontaneous communication, whether it be news, a declaration of love, or a thank you, is much more meaningful than the kind a child is *forced* to make.

Another reason for a young child's occasional reluctance to speak is his possible lack of confidence in the verbal area. You know from your own experience that when you are reluctant to do something (say, dive off a diving board), it may be because you are afraid. With a preschool child, a reluctance to talk may also arise from the fact that he doesn't have the words or he just prefers to become involved in something without talking about it. With our adult emphasis on verbal skills, we sometimes forget to really enjoy doing something without speaking. This is particularly true for a child who is just learning to use language.

Preschool children ask lots of questions. This tendency on the part of preschoolers may be a problem sometimes because of the repetition of being asked the same question or a series of questions or simply because the questions may be difficult to answer. What is the child saying by asking all those questions? He may indeed be looking for a specific answer, since preschool and kindergarten-age children are notoriously curious. He may also be looking for attention. Asking endless questions is a good way to keep an adult involved. If you recognize that a detailed answer may not be what your child is looking for, you may find it easier to reply. Don't be embarrassed if you don't know the answer to a question like "Why is the sky blue?" or "How do worms breathe underground?" It is a good example for your child to observe that you don't know all the answers. You are also setting up a good example by helping him look it up. Most important is your being honest about not knowing and praising him for a good question, rather than being upset that he has outwitted you by asking you something you did not know.

AN OPEN
COMMUNICATION SYSTEM

There are lots of things that get in the way of developing a good, open communication system in which you and your child are really in touch with one another. A major factor, rather obvious but often overlooked, is the age difference. As we've noted previously, children see things differently and even think differently than adults. This makes it difficult for you to understand them at times, and it certainly makes it difficult for them to understand you. But communication is, after all, a problem for everyone. We hear a lot about the communication problems in marriage, for example, or other situations where adults live or work closely together. Psychologists have discovered a basic reason why many of these communication problems exist: the fact that each person sees things somewhat differently. You probably recall the sociologists' demonstration of how each person seeing a crime enacted in front of a class describes it differently. A related problem is that people seldom really listen to one another in the communication process. Often, they are too busy attempting to get their own point of view across. A third communication problem arises from the fact that much of communication is nonverbal. These are the same problems that tend to interfere with our communication with children. Let's look at some of the ways in which we can deal with them.

Make Your Message Understandable

A major problem for many parents of young children is putting their message in a form that their children are able to understand. Today's children often appear to be more advanced intellectually than they really are because of their sophisticated use of language. As well-known Swiss psychologist Jean Piaget discovered, children's language often develops faster than their ability to conceptualize. Young children also tend to see things from a different perceptual vantage point than we do as adults. For example, they tend to be naturally more egocentric and thus find it difficult to look at something from another person's viewpoint. What this means is that the child may not be able to understand what you are trying to communicate, even though he apparently knows the words. In addition, young children do not have the same capacity for processing information (thinking) as we do as adults. For example, they can't see that something may fit into two category systems at the same time, and they can't deal with abstract concepts.

The difference between adults' and children's thinking and perception can block communication or mutual understanding. For example, the problem of not being able to take another person's perspective until at least age seven makes it difficult for a young child to sympathize with the fact that his mother has a headache or that another child wants to play with his toy. While this may make a preschool child seem selfish or uncaring from an adult point of view, it is actually no more unreasonable than his being unable to ride a two-wheel bicycle at age three or four.

Knowing What Is Developmentally Appropriate

Talking to children requires a knowledge of what is to be expected at their particular stage of development. As we've said earlier, try not to be too formal or to use language that is beyond the child's reach. Most important, keep in mind that communicating effectively with a child is not simply a matter of using a vocabulary that is within reach; it also involves dealing with concepts that are meaningful to the child. For example, ideas such as truth, loyalty, and charity are admirable, but they are too abstract for a young child to understand. You may communicate your adherence to these values by demonstrating specific behaviors that are consistent with them, but you cannot expect a young child to truly comprehend or even behave consistently in accordance with these abstract ideals. We have found that parents who speak at a level that is beyond their child's understanding tend to elaborate on their initial explanation. In most cases it only makes matters worse. The lengthy, elaborate explanations further confuse the child or turn him off.

Demonstrate Whenever Possible

Of course, much of what you may want to tell your child will not lend itself to providing accompanying action. But whenever possible, especially when you are giving directions, try to demonstrate as you speak. Young children find it easier to imitate an action than to follow verbal directions. If you're showing your child how to set the table, set a place for him to imitate rather than tell him, "The spoon goes on the right, put the fork on the napkin," etc. This is not to say that the words may not be helpful, too, but don't leave out the accompanying action if possible.

Avoid Talking Too Much

Sometimes parents get overzealous in their efforts to talk to their children about all of their shared experiences. Verbal stimulation is helpful to children, but don't overdo it. Too much language can be overwhelming to a child. Children need to experience things on their own, at their own pace. A child needs some quiet time to observe and reflect. He may want to point something out to you or ask a question. If you are always the one taking the verbal initiative, he may get lazy and wait for you to tell him what to see, or he may tune you out. In a recent study that we conducted, we observed a mother who pointed out everything that was taking place on the way as she drove her child to preschool. In between pauses she talked about plans for that day and what she and her child had done on the previous day. Her little three-year-old was being bombarded with language. She tried to doze a bit, but occasionally she said something which stimulated her mother to talk even more. It is significant that once this little girl was in her classroom, she hardly spoke at all, although she had great fun exploring and playing. Whether this little girl eventually becomes a talker herself or not, at this time she needs some space to observe quietly for herself.

Use a Natural Voice

When talking to children, it is best to use the same voice as when you are talking to an adult. This does not mean that you shouldn't be friendly and warm in your tone, but you don't have to talk in an artificially sweet voice that adults sometimes mistakenly use with children and infants. By the same token, you don't have to use baby talk. This encourages babyishness on the part of the young child, who should feel comfortable about growing up.

Speak at the Child's Eye Level

Have you ever looked at the world from a child's physical perspective? One of the authors noted that when she took her young child to the zoo and was talking about the giraffe's long neck and the stork's beak, her daughter didn't respond. When she bent down to her daughter's eye level, she realized why. All she saw from that perspective were the animal's *legs*.

It is good to make eye contact when you talk with someone. In order to do that with a young child, you need to sit down or squat. We encourage our young teachers to do this. You'll see that this makes what you have to say more effective in that the child is more likely to respond.

Avoid Sarcasm

As adults we sometimes express our impatience or anger through the use of sarcasm. It is important, however, to avoid this practice with young children for several reasons. Sarcastic language is apt to confuse a young child, since he may take it literally when you may be intending just the opposite meaning. For example, you might say "Oh, great!" when your child spills his milk, or "Nice job." Of course, that's not what you mean. We believe that if you are angry or upset or have some constructive criticism to offer, be straightforward. It is healthier to talk about this directly with your child or, if that is not possible, at least to resist a sarcastic expression of that feeling. In addition, sarcasm may be intended to be funny, but it is a biting kind of humor which is usually hurtful to the person toward whom it is directed. It is certainly not constructive to hurt your child in this way. It also sets a bad example which the child is likely to imitate.

COMMUNICATING IS
ALSO LISTENING

Now that we've explored some ideas about how to be more effective in talking to your child, we should devote some time to the art of listening. Parents often forget how important listening is in the communication process. This becomes very obvious in our experience in helping families that are having communication problems. Frequently their problems are much more severe in the area of listening than in talking.

Listening to a younger child is a different matter than listening to a child who has acquired more adequate verbal skills. When your child has relatively limited verbal skills, you need to be especially patient, because it is very easy to overwhelm him with your language. This is likely to "short-circuit" the communication process, which, of course, is not desirable if you want to keep the relationship a reciprocal one. How can you avoid this? Again, patience is your best ally here. Make a special attempt to "hear" what he is saying. Let him try to get his point across without interrupting him, even if you don't agree. You'll find that holding your tongue isn't very easy, but it is important, since you are showing him respect and providing for him a listening model which, hopefully, he will imitate. It doesn't mean that you have to agree, just accept his right to express his ideas.

When your child has acquired greater verbal proficiency and is more capable of talking back in an extended way, you may find that you are each so busy trying to get your own point across that you fail to listen to one another. This is true for all human interaction (it is a frequent problem for husbands and wives, for example). Ironically, if you devoted more time to listening than talking in that kind of exchange, you would get a better idea of what the other person was saying, and, in the long run, you would probably be more effective when you speak. You will also increase the possibility that the other person would listen to you in turn, especially a child who tends to imitate your behavior.

Of course, your child, or another person, can listen to you without really hearing what you are saying. That is not the kind of listening we are encouraging. To truly hear what your child is saying, you need to allow him the time and space to talk. You also need to take in what he has to say nonjudgmentally, at least at first. This is not easy to do, suspending judgment for a while. Concentrate on trying to hear what's being said and on understanding the message. Adults have a habit of jumping to conclusions about what children are saying. Since your child is younger than you and has a different point of view and a different way of thinking, it's all the more reason for listening carefully.

Paraphrasing

How good a listener are you? Are you better with adults than with children? Do you have some special problems listening to your own children? A good technique for testing your ability in this area and improving your skills is *paraphrasing*. This technique involves listening to what your child is saying when he is telling you about some experience and periodically repeating in your own words what you thought he said.

For very young children it is mostly a matter of using your

language to describe their experiences with feelings, much as you would point out any other experience for them. For example, if a toddler falls down and cries, in the process of comforting him you may explain to him that sometimes it *hurts* when you fall down. You can talk to your young baby about feelings of sadness and happiness in the same way as you might point out other experiences that occur. As your child gets older you can encourage talking about experiences involving feelings. By encouraging talking, generally, you will discover that your child is able to talk about feelings and other experiences that you share. One of the best ways to encourage a child's growth in this area is to model the desired behavior yourself. If you are able to talk about your feelings, your child also is more likely to be able to do so.

That's one way of letting him know that you are aware of how he feels rather than attempting to dismiss or deny his feelings. In that sense he is apt to feel safer expressing himself to you. He also realizes that it is acceptable to have those feelings. When you accept his feelings you also need to help him to find appropriate actions. For example, if you help him to recognize that he feels angry, this does not mean that you approve of his hurting anyone. But by allowing him this verbal expression, by offering him acceptance and sympathy and by helping him to find solutions to his problems, you are lessening considerably the likelihood that these feelings and problems will trouble him at a later point in his life.

One reason for the difficulty adults usually have in identifying and talking about their feelings is the fact that they themselves were not encouraged to do so as children. Children are not naturally reluctant to talk about how they feel, but they frequently pick up cues that their parents and other adults are not comfortable when they do so. They need encouragement and experience to become better able to express themselves in this area.

Maintain an Accepting Attitude

As important as your encouragement and mode of talking about feelings is your maintaining an accepting attitude whenever possible. Try to resist jumping in with "if you only . . ." or "You should have . . ." or "Big boys don't cry." That is bound to turn your child—or, for that matter, any person—off. Parents are often afraid if they let their children talk about feelings such as sadness or anger, it will only exaggerate the problem. Quite the contrary is true. As long as they are helped to realize, for example, that talking about being angry does not give them permission to hurt someone else, they are, in fact, less likely to do so than if they keep those feelings bottled up. It works that way with feelings, too, incidentally. You might have had the experience yourself of talking about how sad you felt and finding that you had a sense of relief after you had "gotten it out in the open."

NONVERBAL COMMUNICATION

Listening does not just involve paying attention to language. In fact, a very important portion of communication is nonverbal. How do you become aware of the needs of a child who may be unable to express himself in words? "Tuning in" to nonverbal communication at any age level requires a sharpening of your observational skills. You are paying attention to the visual language instead of the spoken language, but the same principle applies. You need to take the focus off what you want to say for a while and observe or listen to the nonverbal messages that you and your child are exchanging.

If you look carefully, you will find lots of clues as to how your child is feeling in what he is doing as well as in what he is saying. He may talk bravely but give you an indication by how he is standing that he is really afraid. The way he stands or moves, his posture and facial expression—all reveal anger, sadness, fear, confusion, and other feelings. You can help your child to identify and to put these feelings into words.

If your child is an infant, much of your communication is bound to be nonverbal. It is important to talk to your baby, but your physical contact with him is likely to be most meaningful. This physical contact is not only very pleasing to him, but it is also delivering a message. You are telling him that you care about him and that you are trying to meet his needs. This is a good basis for building a sense of security. Research evidence has shown that a child who has been deprived of this kind of close physical exchange in infancy can make this up later in childhood, but it is highly desirable for an infant to receive this type of adult attention in the earliest weeks and months of his life. But the point we are emphasizing here is that the additional communication that you provide in holding and playing with him is also essential. In keeping with what we have said earlier, you are also likely to get more out of this additional contact as well. The baby gives you something in return. You will likely enjoy his smile or touch and the sounds of contentment he will eventually make. If you are just busy caring for his physical needs, sometimes you get to feel like a martyr.

You need feedback from your child to feel good about yourself and to have some idea of how you are doing. Usually, as adults, we can judge the effectiveness of our communication by what the other person says or does in return. With an infant or toddler who isn't speaking yet, you don't get this form of feedback. How do you know what they want or how they are reacting to your response? Most rewarding for you as a parent is likely to be a smile, as we've noted. If your infant has been crying, you get some positive feedback by his change to a more contented state. "Body language" is another important kind of exchange with a preverbal child. The infant's relaxed posture or physical orientation toward you can be informative and, of course, very reassuring and rewarding to you. Children's nonverbal messages frequently take the form of forgetting or "dragging their feet." Another commonly observed nonverbal message is the "stomach ache" before school. Still another, which is very easy to misinterpret, is negative behavior, such as teasing a sister, which is really designed to get the mother's attention. Obviously, just because there is a hidden message, you can't always ignore what is happening on the surface, such as dealing with a child's pain or preventing him from hurting his sister. But it is also helpful to be sensitive to the nonverbal message because, until you discover what your child is really trying to say, you will have a difficult time changing the surface behavior.

From your own point of view, you may be unaware of how many nonverbal messages you do communicate to your child and to what extent they influence his behavior. Remembering again the particular vantage point of young children, you should keep in mind that a child who has a limited understanding of language is very aware of nonverbal communication. Like the tourist who doesn't speak the language, he needs to depend on other clues to discover what you are saying. Is what you are saying and how you behave always in synchrony? What kinds of nonverbal messages might your child be getting? Even a young infant may be aware at some level of the tenseness in your body as you hold him. Although he may not really know that you are frightened or angry, his own body, which is in touch with yours, will sense it. The way you hold your child's hand, your facial expressions, of course, and many other subtle indicators are delivering unspoken messages. This may seem troublesome to you as a parent. You may not be able always to deliver pleasant nonverbal messages, but it is good to be aware of this dimension of your exchange with your child and bring it under control as much as possible.

To take another brief but important example, your nonverbal behavior can indicate whether or not you respect your child. If you insist that he always follow your schedule and never interrupt what you're doing to ask you to listen or to look at something he's done, you're saying, "You're not very important; what you have to say or do isn't very worthwhile." You can tell a child you love him and value him all you want, but if you don't demonstrate it, he is not likely to really believe it.

THE UNCONSCIOUS MESSAGE

Many feelings and other messages are "unconscious" in that you or your child is unaware of the intent of your communication. As we've noted earlier, you may observe your child making a bodily gesture that is inconsistent with what he is saying. How many times have you been in a situation where someone says, "It's no trouble," while they are looking very uncomfortable or annoyed?

In a situation like that, the person may actually be unaware of how annoyed they are. What are we suggesting regarding the possible "unconscious" messages exchanged between you and your child? We don't expect you to try to read into every action that takes place between you or always to search for hidden meanings. It is possible, however, to keep in mind that surface behavior isn't necessarily what it appears to be and that you, as well as your child, may be saying something very important about how you really feel by the way you behave, something that you have never stated explicitly. How can you be more alert to this? All of the points that we have made earlier about sharpening your observation and listening skills should prove helpful in this regard.

Take a look at your own nonverbal communication. How might you be telling your child, without words, that you are angry or disgusted, or that you don't have much confidence in him? Or, to take another typical example, you might find yourself saying, "That's beautiful, dear," in reaction to your child's drawing while, even without your being aware, your tone of voice and facial expression may be saying, "I know you can do better." Children are quite adept at detecting your hidden attitudes; it behooves you to try to be more sensitive to them, too. In the case of your child's behavior, it is very easy to be taken in by things he says or does which may in fact be quite the opposite of what he really means. We've already pointed out that if your child is afraid, he may cover this up, for his sake as well as yours, by acting very brave. In that case, unless you are an astute observer, you may not realize that he actually needs some reassurance or support. Another example with older children has to do with their attitude toward school. Many parents are misled by their children's apparent indifference when it comes to schoolwork and assume that they don't care. Quite the contrary. In many cases, these apparently indifferent children are very discouraged about their ability to do well in school, so they give the impression of not caring. They may be keeping the "truth" about their concerns from themselves, which makes it difficult to help them. But if, as a parent or teacher, you just take them at face value, you can get very angry. It is only by tuning in to their fear or doubt that you have any chance of helping them to drop their guard of indifference.

Verbal communications may also carry unconscious messages that you are unaware of. Many of the messages that you deliver as a parent as well as many of the messages that you receive from your child are unconscious. These messages are usually significant, but at the same time they are usually difficult to understand. The reason for the difficulty in understanding is that often the real meaning of unconscious messages differs from what it appears to be on the surface. In fact, many of these messages are disguised in forms which imply just the opposite of what they actually mean. For example, a child who is being a nuisance may actually need and want your attention. However, because of the unfortunate way he goes about seeking this attention, he may be sent away or punished. By the same token, a parent who is extremely overprotective of a child may actually resent that child or feel guilty about not really liking the child unconsciously. But if the hidden message remains hidden, the problems may get worse instead of better. The child who is being "bad" continues to offend parents he really wants to have love him, and parents who do too much for their child end up with a child whom they resent more than ever for being so helpless and demanding.

Being in better tune with your own unconscious and your child's can improve the communication that exists between you. But there are two cautions to keep in mind:

Leave the psychoanalysis to the analysts. Don't try to be a mind reader or to confront your child with every possible hidden meaning in what he does or says. It is sufficiently helpful to be aware that what is happening may have a different meaning than that which appears on the surface. You might gently suggest that sometimes children get stomach aches when things aren't going well in school or, if that doesn't get some discussion started, check with the school itself about what may be taking place there that might account for your child's reluctance to go. In any case, it is not wise to insist that your child admit that his stomach ache isn't real and that he is having a problem in school.

Don't use your child's unconscious against him. A person's unconscious message can be used against him. Children do that quite often. Your child may detect that you're feeling guilty about having to be less involved with him because of some heavy responsibilities at work. He might take the opportunity to ask you something which he knows you would refuse under other circumstances. Because of your guilt, you may give him the expensive toy or the privilege that he wants. Parents do this to children, too. You may arouse guilt in your child by telling him that he is responsible for your headache, ill health, or even your divorce. This is a good way to keep a child in line, but it does serious psychological damage. Another damaging technique involving the unconscious is arousing a child's deep-seated feelings of insecurity. This is very tempting with a rebellious or apparently independent child. How many parents have threatened such children with sending them away or putting them up for adoption? Of course, the counterpart in children is threatening to run away from home, which is designed to arouse parents' unconscious guilt feelings.

SUMMARY

Communication is a two-way process. As you express yourself to your child and hope that he will understand you, remember that he is also expressing himself and hoping for understanding. Communication is nonverbal as well as verbal. Your feelings are communicated through touching, your facial expressions, and your tone of voice. It also involves listening. Many times communication is "short-circuited" because you are not listening to your child or he is not listening to you. Communication also involves the transmission of values. You tell your child your attitudes and what things you think are important not only by what you say to him, but also by your own behavior and the behavior in him that you encourage.

Suggestions for improving communication include "paraphrasing," encouraging talk about feelings, knowing what your child might be able to understand, not talking too much, using a natural voice, being at the child's eye level when possible, avoiding the use of sarcasm, and accompanying your talking with action when possible. It is also important to be aware of the unconscious message that may underlie what your child says or does on the surface. In communicating rules and expectations, try to make them as clear and brief as possible. Avoid elaborate explanations. Don't expect that your child will always be open to your message or that he will be able to communicate clearly to you. Remember to look for nonverbal clues. As in most matters of child rearing, be patient and understanding, and more than likely the exchange between you and your child will be a reasonably open, two-way channel of communication.

ADDITIONAL READING

GINOTT, HAIM, *Between Parent and Child.* New York: Macmillan, 1965.

GORDON, THOMAS, *Parent Effectiveness Training.* New York: Wyden, 1970.

ROGERS, CARL, *On Becoming a Person.* Boston: Houghton Mifflin, 1961.

chapter seven
PRACTICAL AND CREATIVE EXPERIENCES TO SHARE WITH YOUR CHILD

Dr. Marie Montessori, the well-known Italian pediatrician and educator, suggested that the "frontier conditions" that existed in earlier times provided a natural challenge for children which aided their development into responsible adults.

While economic and technological advances may have increased the standard of living for many families, it seems to have lessened the natural opportunities for children to acquire a sense of independence and of competence. The dilemma facing today's parents is how to provide children with experiences that are meaningful and challenging so that their need to grow up with a sense of being effective human beings is fulfilled. This is a task that requires planning on the part of adults raising children, but it does not require a lot of fancy equipment and is available to most parents who are willing to make the effort.

In this and the following chapters we offer some concrete suggestions for implementing some of the guiding principles that we discussed earlier. In that sense these are some of the most practical suggestions in our book; we hope you will be able to combine them with the ideas we shared with you about development, values, discipline, and communication. Keep in mind that you aren't expected to follow these suggestions religiously. You have your own personal style, your own preferences, and your own particular skills—use them to create unique opportunities for you and your child.

The suggestions in these chapters apply whether you are a parent who is at home or a parent who is working. In the latter case, you may plan the experiences for a caregiver to carry out. If someone else is to share the experiences with your child, be sure to remind that person of developmental expectations, discipline techniques, and ways of encouraging language to enhance the value of the experiences, as well as of appropriate safety practices.

CREATIVITY BEGINS AT HOME

We've started with activities that can be introduced with little extra effort as you are working around the house. Young children like to "share" adult work. You may be surprised to discover that your child enjoys everyday tasks such as sorting laundry, dusting, and cooking. Allowing her to help instead of trying to get her out from underfoot is an aid to her development as well as less of a struggle for you. Some ideas that we suggest may be particularly useful when you are helping your child to bathe or dress. Others apply to when you are taking her on errands in the car, shopping in the supermarket, or waiting in the doctor's office. Some of the activities suggested are for special times that you set aside specifically to be with your child. Sometimes offering a child special time results in her being more willing to allow you some free time while she is playing alone or with friends.

Actually, there are many reasons for involving your child in activities at home, not the least of which is the positive effect it has on the relationship between you. Time spent together in this way promotes many positive values. It demonstrates an adult as a caring, nurturant person, and it communicates to the child a feeling of being worthwhile and useful. It also teaches important self-help skills. In fact, it is these favorable experiences that form the basis of a child's willingness ultimately to get involved in school and in the community, working to counteract the lack of commitment which often arises in young people in contemporary society. To summarize briefly, your child's participation in household tasks at an early age serves at least four major purposes: (1) it helps to keep her out from underfoot, (2) it is pleasurable for her, (3) it gives her a sense of competence, and (4) it gives her a sense of commitment.

According to many observers, including Erik Erikson, a young child seeks opportunities to "do" things as part of the developmental process of acquiring a sense of industry. Studies have shown that when children participate in useful activities at home they become more cooperative and nurturing and develop a sense of competence rather than one of uselessness. Cross-cultural studies support those findings and have established that children can accomplish responsible jobs well at an early age. It is possible that we have underestimated the abilities of our young children.

ACTIVITIES AT HOME ARE LEARNING OPPORTUNITIES

We should keep in mind that all of the child's activities at home represent learning opportunities. Even routine daily activities such as eating, dressing, and helping around the house involve the acquisition of important skills. The child also learns in this way about herself in relation to the family, acquires social skills, and learns about the physical world (how things work, etc.) and her relationship to it. All of these experiences contribute to your child's perception of herself as a valuable, competent, knowledgeable human being.

Let's take a look at a few examples. Children learn about *numbers* as they set the table; they learn about *color* as they help sort the laundry; they learn about *size* and *shape* as you talk with them about *big* brothers, *small* boxes, *round* balls; they learn about *high* and *low* when they try to reach something, *heavy* and *light* as they carry packages, *hot* and *cold* when they have experiences near the stove or refrigerator, *hard* and *soft* when they have the opportunity of seeing and feeling macaroni before and after it is cooked.

Much of this learning takes place naturally. In some cases you may merely provide the setting and support your child's own efforts. In other situations you may need to be a bit more directive, such as when you teach her how to tie shoes, shop, talk on the telephone, or eat. Likely as not, you have already involved your child in setting the table or doing laundry, and it is really only a matter of recognizing that you are providing important experiences and accenting them, when it is appropriate (certainly not all the time). Eventually all of this takes place without much second thought.

SPECIFIC ACTIVITIES TO SHARE WITH YOUR CHILD AT HOME

The suggestions we make here are just that—suggestions, not prescriptions. We recommend that you not attempt to use them all and, above all, that you use your own ideas and inventions first. When considering appropriate activities, you might ask yourself, How can I involve my child so that I can do what I have to and enable my child to share this experience? Take stock of your own household resources and your own talents and interests, and modify the suggested activities accordingly.

Helping around the house is pleasurable for a young child; that is not necessarily the case for a nine- or ten-year-old. Helping gives a young child a sense of usefulness and importance; involve the child in such a way that she is able to enjoy, experience, and feel competent and successful. For those times when you've planned special activities, play with enjoyment and make it a time to observe, to listen, to talk, to relax, and to enjoy and grow with your child.

For the Very Young Child

Until the age of eighteen months or so, a child can only be involved in activities in very limited ways. A baby can be involved by simply holding and tending to her physical needs; taking care of a child's discomforts immediately is a positive interaction at this early age. Since children need and enjoy close physical contact, touch your baby and let her touch you as much as possible. When the baby is awake, it's important to take her around the rooms and place her in different positions in different ways, using an infant seat, a crib, or a jump chair. Talking to the baby as you work around the house helps to provide the human interaction so necessary for growth and development.

From about three months on you may play with a child with her own toys, and by eighteen months she can start to join you in the activities. Toddlers like to take out, unpack, and even help to put away groceries. They also like to get the newspaper, push an elevator button, turn on a faucet, and help to sort the laundry. By age two, your child can be of real help and truly likes to clean the floor of the closet, empty wastebaskets, wipe finger marks, or use the dust mop. By three she can enjoy helping to make beds, to wash windows, to wash the car, as well as to repeat and perfect the skills she has learned earlier. Remember, you are not taking advantage of your child; involving her helps her to feel important, successful, and useful.

Mealtime Activities

You can invite your child to join you as you are preparing meals. Conversing with your child encourages language, sharing thoughts, and concept development. Talking about what you did, what you are doing now, and what you are going to do helps develop an awareness of sequence (what comes first and next). Label what you are doing as you work by talking about processes—"I am peeling," "Now I'm cutting," "Now I'm mixing," for example. Smell the food and talk about smells. Ask your child to close her eyes and smell the ingredients. What are they? How do they smell? You can even set up a special game with strong smells like cinnamon, onion, and cocoa by putting a pinch of each in a piece of tin foil for children to smell. The same kind of activities can be planned for tasting. As you are preparing meals, invite your child to taste some food and guess what it is, or show her what you are preparing and let her taste the different ingredients and foods.

When you are putting away the dishes after meals, encourage your child to help you put them where they belong. You might have her put silverware in the right place by shape and size, the teaspoons here and the soup spoons there.

Cleaning

As you are cleaning or picking up, you can show your child shapes and encourage her to point out shapes around the room. Talk about which things are heavy and which things are light. As you're cleaning, give your child a dust rag and suggest that she dust "under," "behind," or "next to" some piece of furniture, to help her develop an awareness of positional terms.

Laundry Time

Most people sort clean laundry according to whose it is. Before you sort each person's pile of clothes, you can encourage your child to sort the laundry by color, by size, by use, or by kind. Help her recognize the differences in how the fabrics feel—rough, smooth, silky. Talk about which pile has "more" or "less." As you get your tasks done you are also helping your child to become more observant and to gain experiences with concepts such as rough or smooth, more or less, big and little. Since buttons need buttoning and zippers need zippering at laundry time, it's also a good chance for a child to practice developing those skills.

Shopping

Shopping can be a pretty harrowing experience for parent and child, but believe it or not, it can also be both fun and educational for both. A poem by Dorothy Aldis puts it in an amusing way.

MY BROTHER*

Today I went to market with my mother.
I always help her buy the things we eat.
Not sitting in the pushcart like my brother
Who gets our dinner piled around his feet,
I know where jam is, coffee. Bread and butter.
Each thing I bring she says to Davy. "No!
Don't touch that, Sweetie!" Mostly Davy doesn't.
This morning Davy did some touching though.
He spread his hair with cottage cheese all over.
Bit through paper. Gave our ham a chew.
Licked the butter. "Davy!" cried my mother.
She started in to scold my little brother.
Couldn't.
Burst out laughing.
I did too.

Here are some suggestions that may help you and your child enjoy grocery shopping more. Although you may need to allow extra time, this procedure is a lot less time-consuming than struggling with a reluctant child and a lot less damaging to each of you and your relationship. As you walk down the aisles, ask your child to point out certain foods. For example, in the fruit and vegetable aisles you might suggest that your child point out all the orange fruits or all the red fruits. What else can you think of? If you are in the cookie aisle, suggest that your child point out the red boxes, the yellow boxes. In the canned food aisle a child can look for green labels or a specific kind of vegetable. Suppose your child doesn't know color? Then you can point them out. "See, here are the oranges" or "These small boxes are red." If your child knows letters or numbers she can pick those out also. Sometimes children can even help fill the basket. You can give them pictures from boxes or labels of products and ask them to get the items and put them in the shopping cart.

When you return home, your child can help you unpack the groceries and gain concrete experiences with heavy and light and with classifying food to go in the refrigerator or the cabinet. That makes her a part of your homemaking process rather than

---

*Reprinted by permission of G. P. Putnam's Sons from *Hop, Skip & Jump* by Dorothy Aldis. Copyright 1934; renewed © 1961 by Dorothy Aldis.

an obstruction. Your child can also have some fun tracing the shapes of the boxes and cans if she tires of putting things away.

Getting Dressed

Getting dressed can be a problem for children and parents. To help your child dress more independently, you may start by lining the clothes up for her in the order in which they should be put on. It is necessary to allow extra time so your child can have a successful experience without feeling rushed; you should be available for an occasional tug when she gets "stuck." A young child is often ready to pick out certain clothes for herself long before we are ready for her to do so. In the beginning, it is important to limit the choice to which one of two, but usually children dress faster if they have chosen their own clothes. When your child is very young, you can help her with color recognition by talking about the colors she is wearing. You can also help develop memory as well as an understanding of sequence by talking about what you and she did yesterday and what you are planning to do today as you help your child dress.

Bath Time

Bath time is a perfect opportunity for your child to enjoy playing with water and to float and sink toys. Allow enough time for that, if possible, since it's very relaxing for the child. It's also a good time to talk about body parts—arms, legs, elbows—as well as to teach directional terms—for example, "Let's wash *behind* your ears" or "*under* your knees."

Waiting Times

Waiting can be a problem for adults as well as for children. How do you pass the time standing in line or waiting for the doctor yourself? Children need help with waiting. It is useful to carry a bag full of surprises: stickers, tape, scissors, cards, pipe cleaners, and raisins come in handy for both waiting and for trips or visits to homes or places where there are no toys. A mystery bag (similar to the comfort bag) might have some small items, such as a key, a crayon, a penny, for feeling and guessing and later for tracing. Other useful carry-alongs are a deck of cards to sort by color or shape; pictures of clothing and food from old magazines to look at, talk about, and decide where you find them; and a toy and a cup for playing ("Put the toy in the cup, under the cup, behind the cup").

You might also make letters with your fingers or play guessing games such as "play shopping": I need an egg—where can I buy it? Where can I get shoes?" or "twenty questions": "I am thinking of something blue. . . ."

Car Rides and Trips

As in the case of waiting time, advance preparation is invaluable for making the time more enjoyable. As you ride, you can sing simple songs, nursery rhymes, some of your own favorites, as well as read the signs or pick out the letters. The "alphabet" game is fun to play: you and your child first find an "a", then a "b", and so on through the alphabet. A child can also enjoy and learn by playing "traffic": counting the number of cars, noting the kinds or colors of cars, or picking out the numbers on license plates or signs. Still another guessing game which is fun is asking "What would you find in the closet? in the kitchen? in the library?" While riding in a car you can look for the shapes of animals, objects, and people in the clouds. You'll find that it's great fun and a good chance to use your imagination together in this and other games. It's fun to tell stories with silly sentences where one person starts and the others take over in turn. Children also enjoy riddles ("What has numbers on the dial and goes 'ting-a-ling'?" "What is small and furry and goes 'meow'?") The riddles must be simple—the simpler the better.

"Survival" Supplies

It is a good precaution to take along what we call "survival" supplies when taking a trip in the car. Some basics in this category include a small snack, water, tissues, a paper bag, first-aid supplies, and a change of clothes. This kit will save you stops and prevent the child's possible discomfort, in addition to being useful in a real emergency.

ENCOURAGING YOUR CHILD'S CREATIVITY

Creative activities that you do with your child also benefit you as a parent in several ways:

1. They give you a chance to have fun with your child, to watch your child grow and keep the child within you alive.
2. They enable you both to be more flexible and to try new things.
3. They enable you to have a chance to look at the world through a child's eyes and thereby keep "young-minded" yourself.

Creative activities are naturally appealing to children. In addition, they help a child to feel comfortable with novelty and change and encourage the development of an ability to organize things in a variety of ways. From this point of view, creativity is an important quality to develop in a child who is growing up in a world that requires adaptation to rapid change.

Some creative activities that are possible in the house include reading to your children; painting with water, watercolor, or tempera paint; making and using play dough; glueing styrofoam; playing with water at the sink or in the bathtub; using food coloring with water; pretending; singing; dancing; building; doing physical activities together; using found materials (egg cartons, tubes from toilet tissue or paper towels, macaroni, etc.) for a variety of projects; cooking (soups, salads). Children can even peel and cut when they are three or four years old.

In addition, and even more important, what are your hobbies? Do you plant, sew, knit, cook, play cards, do woodwork? For some special moments, invite your child to share your special interests as a creative activity.

HOW TO SHARE CREATIVE ACTIVITIES WITH YOUR CHILD

Story Time

Some parents enjoy reading a story to their child before bedtime as a way of helping a child wind down the day. There are times, of course, that reading a story is helpful—during waiting times or at just one of those "special" moments you and your child have during the day. As we will note in the chapter on trip taking, library visits are a good shared experience, and helping the children select books to take that you can read to them at home feels very important to them. (Libraries maintain lists of books appropriate for various ages and on a variety of topics.)

Water Play

Painting with water helps children develop fine motor skills by holding the brush and gross motor skills by manipulating it. A small paintbrush and a cup of water with paper works well indoors; outdoors, children love a big paintbrush or roller and a big pail of water. You can set them to work and work with them on painting fences, sidewalks, or outdoor furniture. Sometimes children like to hold the brush with water or squeeze a sponge with water to make shapes, letters, or patterns. You might even point out how fast the water dries.

We haven't overlooked painting with watercolor or tempera paint, but in this chapter we are trying to suggest activities for which little preparation is needed and for which you probably have the materials on hand at home.

Children love to use water at the sink and in the bathtub. Their fun and learning can be enhanced in these situations by some simple preparation. Plastic dishes or containers in the sink, some liquid detergent, and a beater can keep children absorbed and busy for a long time. Washing a doll in the sink, especially with you joining in for a little shared play or necessary supervision, is great fun. Mixing food coloring with water is a delightful sensory experience for young children while they also learn about the properties of water.

Play Dough

Children love to make play dough and use it. The recipe is really simple, and the play dough can be stored in a plastic bag in the refrigerator between uses for a very long time. The recipe is two parts flour to one part salt, mixed with about one-third part water with food coloring added. For example, if you use one cup flour, add one-half cup salt, then stir, slowly adding about one-third cup water with coloring in it as you mix. First it will become lumpy, and then as you knead it, it will take on the consistency of clay. If the mixture stays too sticky you can add more flour; if it is too dry, add more water. It is easy and convenient to make play dough in a bowl and use it on wax paper in the kitchen or on a Formica-top table. Using the finished product is fun for the child as she simply manipulates the material. It also develops creativity, allows her to express herself, and shows her that flour and salt can be changed into another material, which for young children is really a science activity (transforming materials).

Cooking

Cooking is a pleasurable and appropriate activity for young children. There is sensory pleasure from working with the food, mixing, cutting, smelling, tasting. There is an opportunity to measure (math) and transform materials (science) with or without heat; it is also a chance to cooperate and participate in the household and feel good through some successful experiences which will then help them develop positive self-esteem. Making orange juice, Jell-o, and pudding, as well as cutting carrots, making salads, and even preparing vegetable soups, are cooking experiences that children enjoy.

Pretend Play

Children like to pretend to be a variety of things, especially animals and other people. As we have said, it's nice to call up "the child within you" and pretend with your child. It doesn't have to be an extended play, but in participating with your child, you model a beneficial kind of fantasy. You also endorse the value of fantasy and play by joining in, and you are able to enjoy it through the child's eyes. Pretending helps children try on a variety of roles and models which are preparatory to imagining future roles for themselves. It is also helpful in practicing social and interpersonal skills.

Music

Sharing music with a child is fun. It is an activity most children love, one that helps them develop aesthetic appreciation, listening skills, gross motor skills, and the ability to play and to keep rhythms. Most children are very enthusiastic about listening to records and about singing as you work or ride in the car.

Dance

Dance is a combination of movement, the release of energy, and body control. Sometimes in school we give children scarves to wave as they dance to a variety of kinds of music, such as "The Nutcracker" or "The Blue Danube Waltz." Music that tells a story, such as "Peter and the Wolf," suggests themes to children that they can translate into creative movement. You can dance with your child to both classical and modern tunes at home.

Physical Activities

It is healthy for both you and your child to share a little time in running, jumping, skipping, taking giant steps, walking over lines, and walking in shadows. Such activities are fun and help to develop coordination and encourage the use of the large muscles.

Building

Blocks are good for children to use, as they help with eye-hand coordination, problem solving, and designing. If blocks are not available, empty boxes from Kleenex, napkins, or cereal; milk cartons; and toothpaste tubes may be used to build with and even eventually to glue together.

Cutting, Gluing, and Pasting

Children love to cut and paste or glue. These are useful activities for helping to develop fine muscle skills, aesthetics of design, creativity (as a child invents different combinations of materials), and problem solving (as a child finds the way to combine materials). Empty toilet tissue and paper towel tubes, egg cartons, styrofoam from packing cases, and leaves in the fall, along with paste, glue, tape, and staplers, are all possible materials to use. Magic markers and crayons are helpful for adding extra decorative touches. Remember again, with young children, the process of doing is important and sometimes more important than the product that results.

SOME PARENTING PRINCIPLES

Here are some parenting principles you may find useful as you share experiences with your child.

Keep the Developmental Level of Your Child in Mind

It often accounts for her behavior, her limited skill, or her inability to understand.

As you plan the suggested activities, for example, remember to consider your child's inability to wait and her short attention span as well as her need to be actively involved.

Be Flexible and Improvise

Much of what you do as you share experiences with your child will be by trial and error. Some activities you try will work at one time and not at another. If a particular activity is not working, stop and save it for another time. What worked for your other children or for someone else's may not be best for your child. While each child is different, each parent is also unique, and, of course, so is the particular combination of you and your child. For example, if an activity is suggested that doesn't please your child, try another variation, or if you lack the exact materials, substitute others. Don't be disappointed if the final product isn't very beautiful or the project isn't completed. In fact, you and your child may share the delight of a table that is set rather imperfectly by adult standards or by a sincere effort made in straightening a room which still needs the finishing touches applied by you.

Be a Participant in Your Child's Play

As we have repeatedly pointed out, children, especially young ones, learn a great deal more from imitating your behavior than being told what to do. Your child's play can benefit from your participation. Try to get involved in crafts, games, and even fantasy play when you are able, although it is important not to take over or compete. You'll find that as you get involved you will share a child's excitement and fun. And demonstrate by your actions that play is fun and a great way to explore and learn.

Keep Some Time for Yourself

Although parenthood does require time and effort, it does not require you to be a martyr. How do you maintain your own time? A brief verbal reminder to your child will often do the trick. "Now it is time for me to work alone or be alone. This is your time to be alone. We'll play together later." Sometimes this takes several repeated experiences, but if you are firm and committed to your own time as well as time for your child, it works. What if you don't feel like playing? If you are not in a mood or you're tired, take a breather and arrange for a babysitter or send the child to a nursery school for part of the day. Don't deny yourself time on your own when you need it.

SUMMARY

What we have done in this chapter is suggest some of the many ways you can share time with your child. Children enjoy and need the opportunity to feel that they are a part of your life as you do household work, and they feel useful when they can be involved in a small way from the beginning. If you keep it fun and don't expect perfection, this cooperative effort can contribute significantly to a sense of purpose which may stay with a child as she matures. In a similar way, creative activities which may be easily done at home not only keep a child occupied but also can be great fun for both you and her. They also contribute to a creative, open spirit, which is a very useful quality for a child to have as she grows up in this complex, fast-changing world.

ADDITIONAL READING

ALDIS, DOROTHY, *Hop, Skip & Jump.* New York: G. P. Putnam's Sons, 1934.

BETTELHEIM, BRUNO, *The Uses of Enchantment.* New York: Alfred A. Knopf, 1976.

BOSTON MEDICAL CENTER, *What Do We Do When "There's Nothing to Do."* New York: Delacorte Press, 1968.

GORDON, IRA J., *Baby Learning Through Baby Play.* New York: St. Martin's Press, 1970

GORDON, IRA; GUINAGH, BARRY; and JESTER, R. EMILE, *Children Learn through Child Play.* New York: St. Martin's Press, 1972.

THE PARENTS' NURSERY SCHOOL, *Kids Are Natural Cooks.* Cambridge, Mass.: The Parents' Nursery School, Inc.

chapter eight
IDEAS AND PLANS FOR SHORT TRIPS AND FAMILY VACATIONS

> If a child is to keep alive his inborn sense of wonder . . . he needs the companionship of at least one adult who can share it, rediscovering with him the joy, excitement and mystery of the world we live in.*

Children, as we've noted in chapter 3, are naturally active and curious. They like to explore, experiment, and find out how things work. We've said that we believe parents must nurture this curious and exploring nature to help their children develop into competent human beings who will survive, enjoy the world in which they live, and be able to make decisions that affect themselves and us in the future. We've also said that our philosophy includes continued growth through exploration for parents too. To paraphrase the opening quote, "If a parent is to keep alive his inborn sense of wonder . . . he needs the companionship of at least one child to help him rediscover the joy, excitement, and mystery of the world we live in and share it with him."

In the last chapter we talked about encouraging exploration and creative activities through participation and activities in the home. This chapter leads us into growth through exploration outside the home, expanding your child's world through a

*Rachel Carson, *The Sense of Wonder* (New York: Harper & Row, 1956).

variety of short daily adventures, planned family trips, or even trips on which children are obliged to come along. These experiences can offer you and your child a simple change in scenery, opportunities for discovery, and increased information. Trips outside the home can be very satisfying for you and your child, depending on your expectations, knowledge of his development, and preplanning.

Although we recognize the importance of vacations without children and time away from children, this book is focused on growing *with* the children, so the vacations we will discuss are those taken with the children along.

The beginning of the chapter concentrates on local trips that you can schedule around your usual daily activities if you are home or, in some cases, on weekends or in the evening if you are working. The later section discusses the longer family-type vacation.

LOCAL TRIPS PLANNED PRIMARILY FOR YOUR CHILD

These local trips are meant for occasions that you have set aside as special times to share with your child when you are not doing your own errands. The time involved may be five or ten minutes or several hours, depending on your schedule, the age of your child, and the activity. Some of the suggestions offered here may seem commonplace at first, but they are not to a child and will not be to you if you look and experience them through your child's perception. Sometimes it's nice to take these trips only with your own child; other times, you may want to take along a young friend or two or another family. A child's development as well as his enjoyment of the experience is often enhanced by having peers along.

It is useful to take tissues, Band-Aids, and a safety pin or two, even for quick trips around the corner or in the neighborhood. If the trip is any further than to a neighborhood place, pack tissues, Band-Aids, a few small treasures, snacks, and perhaps even water and a change of clothes, depending on the age of your child.

Children, from infants to preschoolers, like to look around stores such as supermarkets, laundromats, shoemakers', florists', pet stores, and post offices. Putting money in the machines in a laundromat is a treat for many children, as is watching the clothes spin in the dryer. You are likely to find your child's actions and reactions informative as well as enjoyable to watch.

We have taken children to buy just one vegetable in a supermarket, one stamp in a post office, one fish in a pet store. By age two and a half or three a child can, with some help, pick out one item in a store, be given some money, pay for it, and even get change. You can also window-shop outside the store with a child, or inside down one aisle, looking at all kinds of fruit or picking out favorite toys or cereals, with no intent to buy. The latter suggestion may sound difficult, but if you tell preschoolers that you are just looking this time and do it a few times without buying, children generally accept the practice.

We have found that very often children have not had an occasion to be on a train or a bus or even in an elevator. A bus or train ride that lasts only from one stop to the next is sufficient, although longer ones are acceptable also. On the bus ride, you might point out that the doors open and close, that the money drops in the coin collector, and that the motor makes a roaring sound. *The Big Red Bus,* by Leonard Kessler, is a favorite book of many children and is appropriate to read to children before or after such an experience. When you take a child for a ride on an elevator, you can lift him up so that he can push the button. You can point out the doors opening and closing, the people getting on and off, and the numbers lighting up as the elevator ascends or descends.

Trips to construction sites, libraries, and a parent's place of work are enriching experiences also. In fact, a visit to a parent's place of work is a particularly satisfying experience for children. They really enjoy seeing what's on your desk, meeting your co-workers, trying an office machine. It helps them to understand where you are and what you are doing when you are not with them. Visits to libraries to take advantage of story hours and to take out books to read at home give children an early start in appreciating books.

No less satisfying is a walk around the block, in the woods, near a pond, or collecting "treasures" from the street. What does your child notice on the walk? What do you see as you share this walk with him? Is there a mailbox, a particularly interesting sign, a barking dog, a squirrel, some stones to kick, some interesting insects? You may want to collect some rocks, feathers, or small treasures. Be sure to bring a small bag or you may end up with a pocket full of acorns. Bend down to see how the area looks at your child's eye level. You may be surprised at what you notice from this near-ground-level vantage point.

Trips to the park, zoo, and beach, to visit a friend or relative, or to a picnic are also favorites for some parents and children and can be times for sharing wonders of sight, sound, touch, and smell.

These suggested trips represent only a few of many possible places children enjoy visiting. Where else might you go? In every neighborhood there are places to visit that help a child know his world better, even if they are not the usual and traditional places to visit. Our nursery school, for example, is located on a college campus, and our children come at staggered times. We do not take the traditional trips to the firehouse, bakery, police station, community library. But we can explore the children's campus world by visiting the college library, the offices, the campus post office, the art gallery, the cafeteria, the bookstore; we even ride the elevator. You will be surprised as you look around your own neighborhood at how much there is to explore that forms a part of your child's world, just as the campus, in this case, is the world of these particular nursery school children.

On these nearby adventures one of the most satisfying ways to enjoy the experience is to consider it a truly shared experience. Listen to what your child says, watch his wonder, bend down to his eye level to see the world from his vantage point. These things help you to gain a better understanding of his view of his world and enable you to help him to observe, appreciate, and understand that world as well as renew your own appreciation of it. Children usually have a questioning and wondering attitude, particularly when they are encouraged. You should also develop or renew your own questioning attitude and certainly point out features you think are interesting. As one naturalist suggested, if you look as if you had never seen the object before or would never see it again, it enhances your sensitivity and appreciation of whatever you are looking at.

LONGER FAMILY VACATIONS OR TRIPS

When there are children of varying ages, it is useful to pick a place for a vacation that has something special for each person. Children can, however, gain some level of enjoyment, expansion of their horizons, and sharing time even in places that have not been designed as "children's" places. Sometimes it's a motel room that catches a child's fancy; other times it's a pigeon that he remembers most. We have had success and memorable experiences with our own children in visiting cities such as Washington, D.C., Montreal, and Boston; lakeside cottages in Maine and New Hampshire; tourist areas in Florida and Pennsylvania; child-oriented environments at Lake Placid and Lake George; and historical sites like Washington, Williamsburg, and Sturbridge, in addition to the usual camping trips and visits to see relatives. When the children were quite young, just going down the motel hall to get a drink out of the machine and some ice was exciting. In one motel it was the slide into the pool. In Boston, for example, the preschooler liked the ducks and the swanboat in the Boston Common; in Sturbridge it was the home-baked cookies in the outdoor kitchen.

We have found that important prerequisites to some memorable experiences on trips are (1) doing advance research of the area you are planning to visit to discover what family members might like; (2) balancing what you would enjoy with the limitations of your child's stage of development; (3) expecting and understanding that there will be frustrations, stresses, and mishaps when you travel with children; (4) determining what you will do to lessen the frustrations, first through anticipation and then through handling them when they occur; and finally (5) as adults, sharing the wonder of the experiences with your child.

GENERAL PLANNING
FOR TRIPS

How do you plan for trips? You might begin by asking yourself: Who is the trip for? What do you expect for yourself and the children from this trip? What do you need to do to enjoy the trip? What might the children like in this particular place? What are the absolute essentials you must plan for?

In some cases, the decisions about the trip may be pre-determined by economics, time, or age of family members. If there are options available, planning the trip with your priorities and your understanding of child development in mind is likely to make the trip more enjoyable. Here are some examples of specific kinds of questions you might need to ask:

Where do you want to stay? A motel, a cottage, a farm-house, a tourist home? Each location has some advantages and some limitations. Cottages or vacation sites with more than one room allow for some separation and privacy that is often much needed on a vacation. Families generally expect that everything will be smooth for seven days and seven nights, or however long the trip is, forgetting that at home they rarely spend such concentrated lengths of time together in such close quarters.

Do you expect to cook and/or clean? That is generally a feature of many cottages and farmhouses, but not motels. Cooking can save money, but it's not much of a vacation for the cook; yet young children often have particular and limited preferences, short attention spans, and limited waiting ability. While restaurants may be the favorite choice of adults and older children, the most useful compromises for travel with young children may be planning on bringing a young child's food along, breakfast in the room, and picnics or packed lunches and suppers.

On one of our first trips with an infant and a three-year-old, we went to a motel because we did not want to be responsible for cleaning. We were lucky and found a motel with a kitchen unit. We didn't want to eat all our meals in, but we felt that three meals a day out with young children was too much for developmental as well as economic reasons.

With whom do you intend to vacation? Your family alone or another family or families? There are real individual preferences here. For some families with two or three children, sorting out the desires and needs of their own family members is complicated enough. Others find that taking along another family nicely dilutes some of the intense togetherness of vacations. One obvious limitation is that there are usually twice as many bathroom trips or restaurant seats needed.

Where are you going? Do you intend to find a vacation in a natural setting or an artificial or city environment? Children have a natural affinity for things in nature. Rachel Carson notes that "those who live with the mysteries of earth, sea and sky are never alone or weary of life." But not all adults have that natural affinity for nature. Young children can also enjoy museum visits, tall city buildings, and rides on escalators.

How will you travel? Car, plane, train, or bus? Short rides on buses or trains may prove to be quite an adventure for yourself and the children. Yet car travel allows you to be more independent of schedules. Economics may be another factor. If economics is not a concern, there are still other questions to consider. How far are you traveling? Can you be together in the car for that long? Are your children good travelers? Where is everyone going to sit? Who is going to drive and who is going to attend to the children?

What we are suggesting by these examples is that it is useful to anticipate what you would like to do, see how it fits with what can reasonably be expected of children based on their development, and prepare and plan based on those expectations.

Practical Planning

Anticipation and preplanning help make a trip relaxing and enjoyable. Attending to some basic practical considerations can prevent unnecessary crises that may take the pleasure out of a trip for you and your child or children.

For example, children always seem to get thirsty in the car. For some people it is easier to plan to carry a thermos of water in the car than listen to a whining child. Others say that such pre-planning interferes with spontaneity. But planning need not interfere with spontaneity if you retain a flexible attitude that allows for changing plans and acting on good ideas of the moment, even regarding a thermos of water.

Suppose the jog or thermos of water is in the car, but you see water fountains that the children want to try out. What is the harm of altering the plans and stopping for drinks from the fountains? Or suppose you've prepared a picnic lunch for the trip but pass a most unusual restaurant. You could certainly decide to eat at the restaurant for lunch and picnic at another meal.

When we first began to make trips with the children, we planned down to the very last item and made lists for everything we had to take. Each subsequent trip became much easier; we had our lists and could pull them out to be modified for the current excursion. The kinds of lists we prepared included clothing lists for each member of the family, toy lists, emergency lists, medical lists, and food lists. We also made lists for particular sites. For example, if we were going to be at a beach, there were certain supplies such as suntan lotion, thongs, and big beach towels that we needed. If we were going camping, we needed mosquito repellant, candles, a cookstove. There were weather-related lists, too. One was a list of essential rainy-day gear, another a list of clothing for vacations in the snow. There was also a specific list of things to take in the car and one for games to play in the car. The car lists included pillows for the children, water, snacks, changes of clothes, tote bag for each child. Car games included picking out alphabet letters, finding animals and houses, and singing, as well as others listed in chapter 7. Surprise bags for the children were packed with stickers, Scotch tape, cards, miniature dolls, dinosaurs, magnets, and special favorites. Waiting time supplies that came in handy in restaurants included family photos, pencils, a couple of crayons, and pocket-size toys to manipulate. Other waiting suggestions were noted in the last chapter, including finger play and other games that require no materials.

Developmental Considerations

There are some developmental factors that are helpful to keep in mind regarding trips:

1. Trips and excursions demand a higher degree of control and inhibition from a child. As parents, we do well to minimize stress by having water and snacks on hand.

2. For some children who thrive on regularity and routine, eating, stretching, and riding in two-hour cycles is useful. Naturally, there are other children who can go for hours without stretching or needing a bathroom, and sometimes it turns out to be the adults who need relief soonest!

3. Children seem to become more demanding and regress somewhat on trips. Some will not go to the bathroom in strange settings and are suspicious of new foods or strange beds. At ages one to three, children are particularly suspicious in that way. At three to six years old, being more adventurous, they are less likely to have that problem.

4. Some children have trouble going to sleep when they first enter new quarters; they need time to explore. It may be useful to plan to stay in at first to help them over anxiety, newness, and strange noises.

5. A sling or backpack is a convenient way to carry an infant. It allows you freedom of movement for your hands and allows the child to be close to you and move his head and his legs. One caution here: if your infant is on your back facing backward, make sure he is checked often to see how he is doing. He may be touching things on the wall behind you, as one of our children did, or disturbing people in line behind you.

6. For a six- to eighteen-month-old, a harness provides safety while allowing active movement. For children even up to five or six, a portable stroller is useful for times when they can't or don't want to walk anymore.

7. When planning sightseeing, it is helpful to try to keep the developmental needs of children in mind—their short attention span and need to touch and explore, for example.

8. Sometimes we have our own expectations of what children will like and are disappointed when their favorite part of a trip turns out to be something altogether different. In our eagerness to be good parents and give children all the experiences we sometimes overlook children's span of attention, developmental factors such as what they can see at their eye level, and their related experience. What he favors most may be what he can see best or

something that is closest to his experience. For example, a three-year-old in the zoo may simply want to watch the pigeons. In one case, a child went to the Empire State Building in New York and wanted to watch the mail chute the whole time. Or, with his short attention span, a child may be finished sightseeing in fifteen minutes whereas you wanted to show him the whole zoo. Other times the motel is the child's favorite place, and he would rather stay there than do any sightseeing or wandering.

9. In some places children have to be supervised carefully as well as reminded about looking rather than touching. This may occur on some trips, but also when visiting other people's houses, an antique store you wanted to browse in, or a home filled with small, inviting, but breakable glass animals. Although most of the time your supervision and reminders will work, sometimes it requires too much restraint for a child, and you are best planning that experience without the child.

10. Sometimes the family has to go on a business trip or visit someone in a location that is really not appropriate for a child. In those cases, preparing a bag of the child's materials and activities is a most important part of anticipation and planning. A helpful bonus is to spend some time before or after with your child in some activity for him. You might also investigate to find out whether in the locations that you must visit there is something a child can enjoy.

ENHANCING A CHILD'S DEVELOPMENT ON A TRIP

How can you help to enhance your child's development on local trips and more extended vacations?

One way is to have him help in the planning and preparation in accordance with his age. Sometimes a child can pick out one or two small toys from a limited selection to pack in his bag. Sometimes he can just help to place what you've picked in the suitcase. Later on, he may be able to prepare his own bag alone. As he gets a little older, he may make limited choices. For example, he can choose between two shirts to wear or among several choices on a menu. By preschool, children can be involved in actually planning some activities, packing, and using a map.

Finally, taking time as you share the planning and the

experience to listen and talk with your child in a relaxed way gives him the encouragement to ask questions, express ideas, and state opinions. Questions such as "What do you think happens?" and "I wonder why that happens?" encourage him to make suggestions and to feel free to offer ideas and opinions in a relaxed way also.

FOLLOW-UP EXPERIENCES

Follow-up to an experience can be accomplished in several ways. A repeat visit is often a treat for a child. In fact, a few short visits for young children are preferable to a long stay, particularly for local adventures. Children like to repeat happy experiences. Sometimes they do or look at the same thing over and over; other times they see something new each time.

Other kinds of experiences lend themselves to follow-up activities. If a child has been to a play or a movie, sometimes a related record, or storytelling experience enriches the excursion. Sometimes pretend activities with some props to stimulate some of the activities are useful. For example, suppose you took a trip to the supermarket. At home, some cans, a cash register, and a few bags enable the child to recreate the experience with a friend or a parent as a participant.

If it has been a longer, more distant vacation, a repeat visit may be impracticable, but storytelling, dramatic play, and simple remembering talks help emphasize the experience. These follow-ups are not only fun, but they also give a trip, short or long, more lasting significance.

ADDITIONAL READING

CARSON, RACHEL, *The Sense of Wonder.* New York: Harper & Row, 1956.

LANE, CAROL, *Let's Go Touring.* Disseminated by Shell Oil Co.

MICHAEL, HOWARD, *Games to Play in the Car.* New York: Van Rees Press, 1967.

chapter nine
TELEVISION: HANDLE WITH CARE

Today most parents and children cannot imagine growing up without television. Ninety-eight percent of the families in this country have at least one working television set, and some children spend as much as six hours or more in front of that television set daily. In recent years, in contrast to television's early days, children watch television from infancy and come to the experience without prior activities or information to mediate its effects. So much time is spent watching that educators and psychologists have become concerned with its effects on the developing child. Some of the concern has focused on the experience of watching television, although most has been focused on program content.

What does the activity of watching television consist of? Although some children play as they watch and just look up occasionally at the movement and the sound from the screen, others very often sit for long stretches of time, passively absorbing whatever is shown without much moving about or active participation. Some children curl up and suck their thumbs; others just sit with glassy-eyed stares. Some children are exceedingly cranky if you talk to them while they're watching; others don't even seem to hear you. As they sit, staring at the screen, the television continually transmits pictures and words to them. No response is necessary, nor is there even time to make one. Television creates and controls what is presented, the program, the pace, and the amount of repetition. How does that fit with the needs of the developing child?

As you think about answers to the question, you have to consider the age of the child, the experiences she may bring to TV, and the other activities in which she participates. You'll also need to consider your own philosophy and values and what you think is best for your child.

Earlier in the book we talked about how children develop their minds and bodies through active play. We said that to develop their large muscles they need space and repeated opportunities to crawl, walk, run, jump, and ride bicycles. To develop small muscles they need to have repeated opportunities to button, zip, cut, pour, and fold. If you have ever watched a child develop the skill of pedaling on his bicycle, you have probably seen the child riding up and down, up and down, for what seemed like an endless amount of time. During their own play, children are in control of their activities, what they choose to play, the pace, and the number of times they repeat what they are doing. That is very different from what occurs when children are watching television; the television set controls the program, pace, and repetition, often at a level that is not appropriate for a young child.

Language develops through the need to communicate with someone else. There is a reciprocal interaction when you speak and someone answers, and you are thus encouraged to speak again. Again, this is different from the television experience, which transmits words that cannot be responded to, often at an inappropriate level.

Children make sense out of their world as they become directly involved with raw materials, squeezing, building, changing things, and changing them back again. They touch, feel, taste, and smell. They problem-solve to see which way something goes and then invent a new way for it to be used.

Through play with other children they learn to socialize and be part of a group. They also learn about other people's views and experiences. One child will say, "I'm the mommy, I'll cook dinner." The other says, "No, I'm the daddy, I'll cook dinner." Two views of the social world are represented, and children learn there may be more than one kind of family.

Fantasy and role play with other children and adults give children the opportunity to try on adult roles and prepare for assuming them in adulthood. Fantasy and role play also allow children to learn about and express feelings. How does the television experience differ? Television creates for you. With primarily a television experience, a child can only re-create and will not easily develop the ability to engage in original play or fantasy. In general, then, television watching limits the time a child has to engage in physical activities, to socialize with other children, and to manipulate materials.

TELEVISION PROGRAMMING

What do children understand about the pictures, stories, and information transmitted on the television? Until about age six, children believe what they see unless there is someone to contradict the perceptions. They are not able to distinguish easily between what is real and what is make-believe unless it is they who have created the play. In the case of television, of course, someone else has created the program.

There are also many stories that children do not understand because they do not understand about part and whole. They have no real concept of beginning, middle, and end. Very often the language used is too remote from their level of comprehension, or their understanding of a concept is not well developed. How do you think children internalize the repeated visual experiences of an animal in a cartoon who dies many times and gets back up, or gets hit on the head with no visible sign of pain? Here is an anecdote that illustrates the confusion that television can create. Two young children had an aunt who died around the same time as Grandpa Walton. Later they noticed that Grandpa Walton had come back on some reruns. They then thought their aunt would also come back.

Time is another dimension that can be distorted by television. Commercials use super-compressed time: some of them have human minidramas in which problems are solved in thirty seconds. What do you suppose a child begins to believe about how the world works if he has repeated experiences of watching human dilemmas solved in thirty seconds, with no prior experience to mitigate the perception? Think how frustrating it must be to find out that your problem is not solved "poof!"

It has been suggested that TV has "restored a village type of community" by exposing children to a variety of social roles.* We know that children imitate favorite adults and model adult behavior. What roles does television provide for children to imitate? Do you agree with the men's and women's roles as portrayed on the programs your children see? Are the adult images being projected the ones you want your children to imitate? Until recently, most programs ignored minority groups and the elderly. Most of the leading persons were male, and women were rarely seen outside of the home. On other programs adults hit others and win, and aggression is normal. These actions are also accepted by children unless challenged by an important adult.

Jules Henry, an anthropologist, said that Eskimos teach their children to hunt, fish, and survive, whereas we teach ours to consume. One doctor, looking at television commercials in relation to health care, concluded that TV promotes faulty nutrition, poor dental health, a "pill" mentality, and consumerism. Many of our commercials say buy something new, buy something beautiful, rush out and buy. Toy commercials particularly are often colorful adventures and dramas enacted with toys. Battleships blow up in clouds of smoke. There is usually a low-volume disclaimer at the end, but children often do not understand disclaimers and are disappointed when their toy does not work the same way the commercial showed.

The late Dorothy Cohen, a professor of education who studied children and television, suggested that there should be no television or only limited amounts of television for young

*Grant Noble, *Children in front of the small screen,* Communication and Society Series/vol. 4 (Beverly Hills, Calif.: Sage Publications, 1975), p. 11.

children under the age of five in order to allow time for developmental activities necessary in those years. Children need opportunities and time to develop physically, to fantasize, invent, problem-solve, and have experiences in the world with which to be able to compare and objectify the television images. Although we have just touched on some of the issues related to using television as an activity for young children, we think you can begin to consider the role it has in your own child's life and what you should do about it. Parents have asked, Should my children watch television? How much television should my children watch? Which programs should children watch? What can they do if they don't watch television?

Some schools have been encouraging parents to prohibit or seriously limit both the amount of television watching and the kinds of programming viewed. National PTA groups are sponsoring workshops to help parents teach those children who do watch how to watch television. We, too, believe that it is essential to limit TV viewing for young children and to plan for those selected viewing times. We read about one mother who put her television in the closet so that she and her daughter really had to work to take it out and watch. She also set rules for watching television just as for doing chores and brushing teeth, and she described television as being like stories to help her daughter develop the ability to test images against those perceived in real life.

TV GUIDELINES FOR YOUNG CHILDREN

Children Imitate Their Parents' Television Habits

Children model significant others, not only on television but also in their own homes. Do you watch a lot of television? Do you use it as reward and punishment? You will need to reflect on your own television habits in order to be able to achieve any change in your child's behavior.

Parents should choose programs for young children. One person commented that you would not be likely to put a refrigerator stuffed with fast foods and snacks where your child had unlimited access to it. Why would you give them unlimited access to television? The level of many programs is inappropriate for children. It is useful to watch the program yourself first. Although you won't always know what the next episode will be like, you can get a sense of the format, content, and philosophy of the program in general.

Eventually children can participate by looking over the week's listings with you in advance and agreeing on the programs they will watch. This gives them more of a part in decision making and will probably make them more accepting of the limitations.

Teach Critical Viewing

Children believe what adults say on television and are likely to internalize the behavior and attitudes they are exposed to unless someone discusses these things with them. Even at a young age, children should be taught how to view programs critically. For that reason, when you watch television with your child, it is important to discuss programs, commercials, and your beliefs at an appropriate level with her. In addition, viewing and talking about a program tends to break the hypnotic influence television is apt to have and enriches the experiences presented on the screen for the child.

Limit Television Watching

We have already discussed activities that you can do at home and opportunities for exploring in the neighborhood and outside of your local community. In addition, publishers have recently prepared books on alternative activities and families' use of television; some of these are listed at the end of this chapter.

Your decisions in regard to television and your young child ought to be made based on your child's development, your values, and your needs. When considering how much she watches, consider what else she does. When selecting the programs she watches, consider the values and philosophy you are trying to impart. We note that this is one of the times parenting becomes more difficult. There is no easy answer.

It is so easy to turn on the television set and tell your child to sit there. Sometimes it's the only time your child does sit. Other times you are just exhausted and you know your child will stay put while you rest. Sometimes, as with the difficulties presented by discipline, parents want to be liked by their child; sometimes it is tempting to give in to the rationalization that "all the neighbors' children are watching." We are not saying that television in modest doses will devastate your child, but we are cautioning you not to use it habitually.

ADDITIONAL READING

DEFRANCO, ELLEN B., *Alternatives to TV.* Englewood Cliffs, N.J.: Prentice-Hall Learning System, Inc., 1977.

KAY, EMILY, *Family Guide to Watching Television.* Newtonville, Mass.: Action for Children's Television, 1974.

NOBLE, GRANT, *Children in front of the small screen,* Communication & Society Series/vol. 4. Beverly Hills, Calif.: Sage Publications, 1975.

WINN, MARIE, *The Plug-in Drug: Television, Children, and the Family.* New York: Viking Press, 1977.

chapter ten
NONSEXIST CHILD REARING

A nonsexist orientation is based on the premise that children have a greater chance to maximize their potential as human beings if they are not pigeonholed into gender-stereotypical behavior but are instead encouraged according to their natural preferences. Practicing nonsexist child rearing involves exposing your child to experiences and opportunities for development in a wide range of activities, including those that have been traditionally designated as exclusively male or female.

All children are individuals. Some are assertive, some are passive. Some children are active, others more sedate. Is this because of their sex? As we begin to give boys and girls equal opportunities to be themselves, we discover more and more that although some girls like to sit, many other girls are on the move from the time they are infants. These active girls, whom we may have formerly regarded as not being very "ladylike," love to explore—reaching, crawling, and then walking, running, and falling. By the same token, some boys are fighters who will give you an argument or a struggle from the beginning, while other boys are much more gentle and also like to sit. Whether or not gender is a factor, we know that the range of personalities is not confined to one sex or the other and that we can encourage our children according to their natural preferences and make the most of their individual potential rather than restricting them according to sexual stereotypes.

Parents who practice nonsexist child rearing would, for example, buy balls and blocks for their daughter to provide her with opportunities for early motor development, even though these were formerly considered to be boys' toys. Similarly, they might give their son a doll to play with and crayons to draw with to enrich his experience and encourage him to explore these areas, even though these activities were not typical of what little boys had been offered in the past.

A nonsexist parent model is also important throughout the child-rearing years. To the degree that husbands and wives are able to share child care and household chores, their children are learning a new style of living together that is likely to be useful for the society in which they will live. Nonsexist child rearing tends to fit well with working families and single-parent families where less traditional roles for men and women are likely to be observed. But even in a traditional family it is useful to see which of the stereotypic patterns may be modified according to adult temperament and disposition in order to allow children and adults to experience a more complete set of options.

Nonsexist child rearing also enables parents to broaden their own experiences as they raise their children. The orientation stresses that both parents may take care of children and both parents may earn money, not that fathers work and mothers stay home. Thus, fathers may nurture and care for their children to a greater extent than has traditionally been the case. They may become more active participants in household activities, less helpless than the "bumbling father" that was so often represented. At the same time, a woman may mother and retain personhood simultaneously.

On the other hand, child rearing based on sexist practices occurs when you restrict your own roles to those traditionally defined for mothers and fathers and restrict your child's activities if they do not conform to the traditional areas that have been open to boys and girls. This sex-role bias is a very pervasive attitude which is difficult to eliminate completely even in the most conscientious of parents. Sexually stereotypical behavior tends to be involuntary on the part of both parents and children, frequently unconscious, and in that sense automatic. The result is a lack of openness to certain experiences because of a social convention.

Certainly fathers have been competent homemakers and mothers have been successful in the work force. Certainly boys are just as likely as girls to be frightened, sad, or hurt at times and want to cry, but they tend to feel troubled about expressing these feelings, especially if they have been reminded, "Big boys don't cry." We have frequently seen the restricting effect of stereotyping in nursery school where many boys refuse to try painting or dancing, while girls often will not build with blocks or try woodworking.

Whether or not you regard yourself as a traditional parent, you may see the value in trying to increase the range of possible self-expression and self-fulfillment for both your sons and your daughters. Nonsexist child rearing is a way to offer girls opportunities in sports, higher education, professions, and business that have been traditionally reserved for men. In her book *Nonsexist Child Raising,* Carrie Carmichael reminds us that boys as well as girls are liberated by a nonsexist approach. For example, she asks whether softness and compassion should be qualities reserved for girls. Restrictions have been lifting for men, including opportunities to participate more actively in child rearing.

Carmichael makes a number of other interesting points in her book. One example she cites is the traditional preoccupation that girls have had with their looks. She notes that girls are frequently dissatisfied with some aspect of their bodies, which makes them feel inferior. They may not like their nose, their hair, their breasts, or other parts of their bodies and feel that they are imperfect. Many of these seeds of self-dislike are planted quite early and hamper a young woman's later development. This, of course, is another strong argument for changing the orientation in raising girls. If girls and young women are encouraged to develop other interests and competencies they will need to rely less on their looks for approval.

How can you tell whether you are practicing nonsexist child rearing or child rearing based on a sexist orientation? Treating our children according to sexual stereotypes has been culturally ingrained in many of us. In order to begin to raise children without a sexist bias you have to become conscious of where your biases exist. Since you promote the values of your children intentionally or otherwise, it is important to be vigilant about your own attitudes and practices if you wish to change the pattern. Here are some areas to consider.

PARENTING PRACTICES BEGIN AT BIRTH

If the father participates in the childbirth process and the initial care of the infant, he is exposing his child and the family to a new role of the father from the start and a beginning pattern of nonsexist child rearing. But if the mother always feeds, bathes, and otherwise cares for the baby, this is more of the traditional mother's role. This model of parent participation or nonparticipation in child rearing and household activities affects both daughters and sons. Sons of nonparticipatory fathers, as they mature, typically refuse to do things that they have come to regard as female; while daughters not only are likely to be stereotypic themselves, but are also likely to exclude their husbands from activities that they view as female, including caring for the baby.

Decorating Your Baby's Room

All children benefit from bold colors and stimulating patterns. If you have decorated your baby's room in bold, interesting colors and patterns, you have moved in the direction of nonsexist child rearing. If your rooms tend to be blue for boys and pink for girls, you have stayed with the traditional sexist pattern of bold for boys and quiet for girls.

Dressing the Children

Children are most comfortable in loose-fitting, sturdy overalls for play. If you dress both your daughters and sons in sturdy overalls with bright colors, you are moving in the direction of nonsexist child rearing. If your son is wearing sturdy overalls that are easy to crawl and play in while your daughter is wearing frilly dresses, you may still be following a sexist child-rearing pattern.

Handling the Children

Here are some questions to raise for your own self-examination. How do you handle your new baby? Do you play in a more rough-and-tumble way with your boy infant and a more cuddly manner with your girl? Do you kiss and hug your daughter more than your son? How do you react when they get hurt? Do you expect your small son to grin and bear it but hold your daughter close to comfort her? How do you describe your children? Which child is pretty, brave, helpful, strong, creative?

Children's Play

How much freedom to explore and play independently do you give each child? Does this differ according to the child's sex?

Girls were traditionally kept closer to home, which of course restricted their experience. All young children need space to explore and develop their natural initiative for physical and intellectual exploration. While children differ in their sense of adventure and interest in exploring near or far, as we said earlier, this seems to be based more on individual personality qualities than on male-female distinctions.

What activities do you encourage your young child to participate in? Does your son help in the cooking or dusting or sweeping? Does your daughter rake the lawn or wash the car with you?

What toys do you buy for the children? Have you been able successfully to overcome advertising stereotypes which suggest action toys for boys and dolls for girls? Do you encourage your daughter's athletic interest? Have you given your daughter tools to use? How do you feel about your son's playing with dolls?

In past years, girl have been limited in their opportunities to engage in sports that help to develop their large motor skills. They have also been restricted in motor exploration opportunities that occur through bicycle riding and playing with trucks and cars. Consequently girls have tended to have less well-developed spatial relations concepts than boys. Girls have also generally been discouraged from work in mathematics and science. On the other hand, boys have been discouraged from displaying feelings which has restricted their opportunities for learning how to express these feelings and to acknowledge and deal with them. Boys have also tended to have fewer opportunities for developing verbal skills. In addition, they have tended to have less opportunity and encouragement to develop their small-motor skills than have girls. Boys also need experiences in activities such as stringing beads and using lacing cards.

Feelings

Do you expect your young daughter to be more cooperative and allow your young son to be more assertive? All children need to learn at an early age the appropriate ways to express their feelings and ideas even when these feelings are not always pleasant or when their ideas are different from yours. Traditionally, women have not been encouraged to express their feelings or ideas if they differed from parents', while expressing anger and standing up for personal values were more acceptable for men. Clearly it is a necessary skill for all self-respecting people, one that is difficult to develop if you have spent a childhood being told it is unacceptable.

SOCIETY'S INFLUENCES ON NONSEXIST PARENTING

After you have resolved your own attitudes and practices, there are other factors to consider in trying to maintain a nonsexist child-rearing model. Children's experiences outside the home are very influential. Sexual stereotypes are to be found every-where. A major source of information and values for children is television. Extremely persuasive television messages enter your home, and television programming is replete with sex-role stereotypes. What are women depicted as doing on the reruns that appear all day? Advertising has become somewhat less sexist very recently (it sells products), but mother is still very excited when she is able to produce spotless glasses or elimi-nate "ring around the collar" and toilet-bowl stains. Men in a TV commercial usually drink beer, look helpless in the kitchen or laundry room, or are being fed something for their approval. And the ads still show boys with active toys such as trucks, "action figures," and sports equipment, while girls are expected to love "Barbie," "Baby Alive," or a doll with hair to comb.

A systematic review of children's books, especially early readers, shows the same sex-biased orientation; girls are de-picted as passive, while boys are active, Picture books and readers show Dick doing things while Jane watches. Schools are beginning to weed this sexist bias out of material presented to children, but teachers still find it difficult not to call on the strongest boys to help move chairs or to change the pattern of the girls' playing in the miniature kitchen while the boys build with blocks.

In her book on nonsexist child rearing, *Right from the Start*, Dr. Selma Greenberg suggests that the sexual bias ob-served in schools and other of society's institutions may be viewed as a political battle. She recommends that parents as-sume an assertive attitude to force schools to change their traditional attitudes by promoting a change in policies. Teachers' attitudes are a major factor in creating a nonsexist classroom. Recent studies observing preschool teachers' reactions to chil-dren who get hurt reveal that most frequently boys are guided into activities when they fall or get upset, whereas the teachers tend to keep the little girls near them until they calm down. The teachers themselves are unaware that they have treated the boys and girls differently. At an older age, girls are now being offered shop classes and boys are encouraged to take cooking or what is sometimes euphemistically termed "bachelor survival."

In chapter 15 we discuss the importance of parent advocacy. Nonsexist child rearing requires that you be an advocate for your child's right to fulfill his or her highest potential by eliminating wherever possible the vestiges of sexism in our culture. It begins with identifying the sexist biases that might still exist in our own behavior and attitudes. By reducing the limitations that may have restricted your own behavior to conform to a sexual stereotype, you are making a very important step that will contribute to your own growth as a person as well as to your child's. By your choice of toys, books, and even the TV programs to which your child is exposed, you can further promote a nonsexist orientation. In your selection of a preschool, your intervention with relatives who may be sexist, and even your concern about school curriculum and early reading textbooks, you can also make a difference. Admittedly, it takes a great deal of conscientious effort to develop and maintain a nonsexist orientation. We believe that the increased options that nonsexist child rearing provides your child makes this effort worthwhile.

ADDITIONAL READING

CARMICHAEL, CARRIE, *Nonsexist Childraising.* Boston: Beacon Press, 1977.
GREENBERG, SELMA, *Right from the Start.* Boston: Houghton Mifflin, 1978.

chapter eleven
FATHER AS COPARENT

This chapter is about fathers as coparents. Fathers are beginning to assume a more important role as parents in terms of their direct contact with children. The stereotype of father as a distant authority figure has lost a great deal of ground in this culture during the last generation of child rearing. Just as women are gaining the option of taking their place alongside of men in the marketplace, men should also have the option of assuming a more equal share of responsibility at home. Fathers can become quite effective parents if they are willing to try and if they are allowed to do so.

Even before a baby is born, the "expectant father" can be an ally to the expectant mother who is carrying the child, which, after all, is the product and the responsibility of both of them. Father should be encouraged to read about child care, especially in infancy, along with the mother. It is a good idea to discuss the suggestions offered by the "experts" because in the long run, as parents, you are the ones who must make the final decisions about how to raise your child. This type of shared reading and discussion is also a good way for two parents to bring out their own individual points of view so that some of the possible differences in philosophy can be worked out in advance. It is interesting to note that in spite of the enormous importance of the task of child rearing, parents often spend less time in exchanging ideas and planning in this area than they do in decorating the living room or nursery.

Fathers also need to get involved in the birth process itself. No longer is it generally advisable for the father's role to be to boil water to stay out of the way or to pace nervously in the hospital waiting room while his wife lies alone or with relative strangers in the labor room. The Lamaze method of natural childbirth has offered fathers a role to play and enabled them to be a part of the labor and delivery process. But now even couples who elect not to have their child by natural childbirth are becoming more informed about the birth process together and electing to have the father present during the process. Current research suggests that fathers and mothers who are both involved in delivery (which means that mother is less drugged and father is present) have a special feeling for their newborns. This immediate bonding reaction, roughly akin to imprinting in animals, seems to create a long-lasting attachment between parent and child. The father's presence during delivery also seems to create an important husband-and-wife bond as well.

Hospitals are beginning to accept the value of the father's involvement in the birth process and are relaxing rules which have traditionally excluded fathers from anything other than seeing their newborns through the window in the nursery. Many hospitals now suggest that fathers do the evening feeding while the infant is in the hospital and are much more liberal about visiting by siblings.

Once the baby is home, the father's involvement should not lessen. It is particularly important that both parents keep in mind each other's needs as well as the needs of the other children, if there are any.

The parents' sleeping, eating, and social activities are likely to be altered, which might irritate the father and distance him from the child care process. Ironically, the most successful antidote to this danger is the father's continued involvement with the mother in the care of the newborn. It is generally a mistake for the mother of a new baby to attempt to "shelter" her husband from this responsibility. On the other hand, it is just as disastrous for a mother to hand her baby to the husband as he comes in the door from work and say, "Here, take him, I've had it." Fathers can easily become comfortable handling their babies, just as mothers do, and seem to enjoy it at least as much. If the baby is not viewed as an object in a tug-of-war as to who's responsible for care, both parents can learn to enjoy playing with the baby as well as diapering, bathing, comforting, etc.

The father's role with a newborn does not end with his participation in the care of the child. At that time, the mother is likely to need some extra attention as she is contributing her physical and emotional resources to the new baby. The older siblings are likely to need some extra attention from father also. It may sound to you that the father at this stage in the child's development will not know which way to turn. It can be rather chaotic and exhausting, but all of these needs do not require separate action. For example, the father may take the older children to the park or the circus, creating a special time for them and at the same time allowing the mother some rest or solitary time with the newborn, and this should be an enjoyable experience for father, too!

Of course, the infant needs other things besides attention to his physical needs. Here again, father has a significant role to play. The stereotype of "maternal instinct" and of babies' having a natural preference for their mothers has been discounted by observational studies. Two psychologists, Ross Parke and Douglas Sawin, observed fathers interacting with their newborn babies in a nursery. They found that whether together with their wives or alone, the fathers were just as nurturant and stimulating to their infants as the mothers. Actually, the fathers were more likely than the mothers to hold the babies and look at them, although they did tend to smile somewhat less at the babies than did their wives. Equally as important, infants responded just as positively to their fathers under these conditions as to their mothers. The difference in the actual home situation, of course, is that it has been the mother who has traditionally been the parent who has done most of the handling of the baby, but inherently there is no difference between a man's or a woman's capacity for caring for an infant. Both parents are equally effective and equally as desirable from the point of view of the baby.

Fathers as well as mothers prove to be an important source of stimulation and encouragement for the growth of their babies. Father presents himself as a different stimulus than mother, and this interests the baby. The baby then becomes more familiar and more comfortable with the father. This is important even though he may be less involved with the baby's daily care than the mother. Research has shown that babies as young as five months old are generally calmer when their father has been involved with their care and has played with them. The interaction between father and baby has its practical side, too. It may take place when mother is involved in household tasks or helping older children with homework. It is the letter and spirit of coparenting.

A very significant basis for children's learning is *modeling*. As children's capacities and tendencies to imitate parents and other adults increases, they become better observers and acquire the responses that allow them to copy adult behavior. It is apparent that fathers, through their involvement with their children, provide a model for the children's development. Parents not only model behavior for their children to identify with and imitate, but they also model values and beliefs. A significant aspect of parent modeling revolves around sex roles. This refers to attitudes and behavior having to do with the sex of each parent. In traditional society, where sex-role distinctions have traditionally been very important, the father demonstrates for his sons and daughters how a man in that society is supposed to behave. Sex-role modeling remains a significant aspect of a father's contribution to his children's development, even though in contemporary American society the distinctions between the sexes in terms of role behavior is becoming less pronounced. A father demonstrates a style of behavior that may be unique to him, but to the child it is also representative of his gender. Research to date has indicated that fathers continue to have a special quality to provide as role models which is likely to be more favorable if they are involved and supportive than if they are distant and demanding in an inflexible way. Even at a time when we may be moving toward a more androgynous model presented by both father and mother, just the fact that they are two different adults representative of two different genders seems to have an impact on the child's identification process. Certainly, a father can demonstrate qualities that heretofore have been attributed to women, and in doing so he makes clear to both his sons and daughters and men can be nurturant and emotional as well as objective and assertive. Psychologists Parke and Sawin to whom we referred earlier also noted that fathers tend to contribute to their children's intellectual development through active play, while mothers generally contribute more in the area of language. But, again, even if these distinctions disappear, father and mother both have their own unique qualities to impart as individuals and as representatives of a gender.

There are many ways that a father who may not have the primary responsibility for the daily care of his preschool child can get involved, and not just in the recreational area. He may choose to cook breakfast on Sunday morning and share a special time with his son or daughter while mother sleeps late or has an opportunity to have a meal prepared for her by her husband and child. This is obviously good for her morale and is an excellent model for the child. Typically, mothers make many of the educational decisions when their children are young; fathers should not abdicate this role. If there are two parents at home—or, in cases where parents are separated or divorced, whenever possible—educational planning, including choice of preschool, should be a joint one. Later in this book we provide a more complete discussion on how to select a preschool; at this point we are simply emphasizing that fathers should actively participate in this decision. Not only is the choice of preschool an important one in its own right, but it also serves as a precedent for many other decisions in which fathers have a very active role to play.

Fathers need to assert their prerogatives and to assume their responsibilities as parents when their children are young rather than wait until the children are older. By truly interacting with his child and not just being a "good provider" or a "head patter," the father gets a sense of his child as a unique human being and at the same time conveys to the child a feeling for himself as a person rather than as a stereotype of "father." This seems like a much more genuine way to relate and certainly has more validity for today's child.

ADDITIONAL READING

BILLER, HENRY B., *Father, Child and Sex Role: Paternal Determinants of Personality Development.* Lexington, Mass: Heath Lexington Books, 1971.

GOLD, HERBERT, *Fathers.* New York: Random House, 1967.

GREEN, MAUREEN, *Fathering.* New York: McGraw-Hill, 1976.

LYNN, DAVID B., *The Father: His Role in Child Development.* Monterey, Calif.: Brooks/Cole Publishing Co., 1974.

PARKE, ROSS D., and SAWIN, DOUGLAS B., "Fathering: It's a Major Role," *Psychology Today,* November 1977.

chapter twelve
CHILD REARING AS A SINGLE PARENT

Can a single parent raise children successfully? Most definitely. All of the principles that we have offered throughout this book apply to the single parent. By being conscientious, a single parent can successfully attend to children's physical and emotional needs. In fact, in far too many two-parent families, most of the parenting is done by one parent. Keeping in mind that a single parent can do the job, although it is sometimes more difficult, let's look at some of the special issues that apply to single parents.

Although this picture is changing somewhat, the majority of single parents are still women. These mothers are sometimes concerned about the effect of raising their children, particularly sons, without a male figure present in the household. Perhaps having a parent of each sex is preferable for the child's sexual identification, but it is by no means essential. First, the male child will be exposed to men throughout his development. This may be less so for young children, in which case an uncle, a male friend, or even a male babysitter might be provided. If none of these is available, the Big Brother organization may be able to provide a man to spend some leisure time with your son. Second, in these days of expanding roles for women, there is no reason why a mother cannot provide both son and daughter with a

140

range of activities varying from playing catch to camping to bicycle riding to cooking. Nevertheless, it is just as useful if the child of a single parent learns to be comfortable with persons of both sexes. For a young child, being comfortable with a male figure usually does depend on a rather close involvement. In some cases, of course, this may happen through contact with his father on weekends or vacations.

While you are in charge of rearing your children, you are not alone. There are many others, including teachers, librarians, pediatricians, friends, and family who will also participate. This also applies to two-parent families, of course. If you feel that you are doing your job all alone, you may feel overwhelmed, but if you see yourself at the center of a network, the task may seem less formidable. As a single parent, you may have to be more diligent in using the human resources that are available. For example, if your child is on a visitation schedule with his other parent which may affect his behavior in school, then you should be working closely with his teacher. Or, if you have any special concerns that apply to your single-parent status, such as his relationship to the men you may be dating, you might want to discuss this with your pediatrician or your child's teacher. Librarians provide wonderful story hours and film programs for preschool children, and they can suggest books for you to read about single parenthood and books for the children in areas involving many areas of feelings, including separation from the father, the death of a grandparent, and the birth of a sibling.

Friends and relatives can be a big help, too. Likely as not, you will need a break now and then, which cannot always be scheduled. This is only human, and if you had a good two-parent arrangement, your partner might take over for a while. What about when you are a single parent? Who do you turn to for such relief? Your parents or even your in-laws may be only too happy to help out in these situations. It is important that you do not abuse this arrangement if it is available and that you do not allow grandparents to take over completely. This may be tempting if you have willing grandparents, but ultimately it is best if you can stay in charge even if the pressure of things forces you to abdicate your role for a while. Don't buy the idea that since your marriage did not survive, you are a lousy parent or a lousy person. On the other hand, it is important that you get some relief if necessary. It is *not* foolish to admit to friends and family that you might need some help.

Another source of relief for parents, especially single parents, are "mother centers." These centers vary in services offered, but generally they provide emergency child care, a chance to talk to other mothers or to a counselor, and even classes for self-improvement. Some "mother centers" are publicly funded and some are connected to a church, but more and more parents are organizing such self-help groups on their own. Since financial problems often accompany single parenthood, some of the groups have organized clothing exchanges and a barter system for services, including babysitting, sewing, painting, and typing. This can be extremely useful to a single parent with a tight budget.

Sometimes getting together as a group of single parents for discussions and exchanging ideas is helpful. This may be done with a professional leader or on your own. You may want to share experiences and feelings with others who are in a similar circumstance of single parenthood. Here again, you can institute a barter or swap system for exchange of services and clothing.

One self-help group, Parents Without Partners (PWP), is a national organization with local chapters that offer social programs for single parents. The programs are more comfortable for some single parents who are not at ease with the dating scene or who just want to meet other single parents. This group also sponsors family outings for single-parent families where a single parent doesn't feel uncomfortable because he or she isn't with a spouse.

Expect that single parenthood will require some adjustments for both you and your child. Let's take discipline, for example. If you were not the disciplinarian, you may have to become firmer. This is not always easy, since you may not be in the habit of being firm or you may be afraid that if you are strict, your child will prefer the other parent. It is best to set the record straight in this regard. Even if your child is quite young, explain the reason for the limits you are setting and try not to be intimidated by guilt or by the child's declaring, "I like Daddy better." Yet you shouldn't expect exceptionally good behavior from your child at that point as "proof" that you are able to manage on your own. Either extreme is dangerous; letting your child control you because you are afraid to be labeled a bad parent by him or forcing your child to be a model child because you are afraid to be labeled a bad parent by others.

A major adjustment for many single-parent families is economic. If your standard of living decreases suddenly, this will affect you, of course, but keep in mind that your child will also be affected directly and indirectly. Directly, you might simply have less money to spend on "extras," including entertainment. You might have to move into a smaller house, with less space available, or to an apartment where you don't have easy access to the outdoors. Fortunately, most young childen are quite adaptable in this regard, and you and your child may find other compensations, such as more children to play with in the apartment or more excursions to parks and on picnics that your child will probably prefer to movies and restaurants. The indirect effects are more subtle but likely to be more devastating to your child. They have to do with the "emotional climate" that may arise from the financial adjustments you must make. Your own attitude is very critical in lessening potential negative effects from these adjustments. Admittedly, it is not easy to be cheery when you are worried about a child-support check or where the rent money is coming from, but generally it is helpful if you can spare your young child from some of these worries. You don't have to make up for whatever deprivation the child might feel from the losses that occurred by giving expensive gifts and treats. It is quite possible if you are a single parent to "spend" time with your child in activities such as those described in chapter 7 which will more than make up for whatever losses in financial status may have occurred in your lives. Even routine tasks such as cooking, cleaning, and shopping can be fun and a time for mutual involvement, if done with your child in mind. On the other hand, if you spend lots of time worrying and complaining about what you have lost, it is highly likely your child will also feel very sorry for himself.

A major adjustment for many single parents that affects their children is not having another adult close at hand to discuss things with. It is quite possible that a good friend or relative will serve that purpose, but if not, be cautious about using your young child as a confidant. This is not to say that you should avoid having discussions with your child, but keep in mind that your child should not have to share all of your worries or hear how angry you might feel toward your former spouse. Security is still a major issue for young children. If your child detects your insecurity, he may become reluctant to separate from you, to explore the world around him, and to begin to develop a sense of independence.

This brings us to the broader issue of where you end and your child begins. We have talked about "individuation" process at several points in this book. Just as you might have needed to become distinct from your former spouse or from your parents, your child needs to begin to view himself as a unique individual apart from you. Single parenthood makes this process a bit more difficult for him. It will be helpful if you encourage this separateness without pushing it. For example, he may select his own clothes, which might be different from choices that you make. Let him know that that is OK. He might like different foods than you. He can learn to accommodate to you sometimes while you also accommodate to him. He can begin to accept and appreciate diversity.

Still another related issue here is achieving a balance between your own personal growth and development and helping your child to achieve his own optimal development. As a single parent, it is no more appropriate to give up your life to your child's interests and needs than it would be to ignore your child's needs to meet the demands of your own career or education. Giving your child quality time can lead to burnout unless you allow some space for yourself. You can make use of your single status to develop new skills and find some personal direction without hurting your child. On the contrary, by becoming more aware of yourself and developing your own life separate from your role as a parent, you are maximizing the possibility of your child's being able to develop as a person distinct from his role as your child. If you are too dependent upon one another, chances are neither of you can grow sufficiently. If you are judicious about seeking a substitute caretaker or a group setting for your young child, on the basis of the criteria in chapter 14, you can use that "space" to find your own direction. You are also allowing your child to have valuable experiences with other adults who can also care for him, thus permitting him to gain some of his own valuable independence.

Research has shown that single-parent families tend to have less consistent times for going to bed, eating, and other daily routines than do two-parent families. This was once thought to be very undesirable. While young children tend to feel comfortable with routines, they do adapt quite well to flexible schedules, within limits. Our own university child care center has adopted a flexible schedule for parents who are going to school and working. Many of the children go to school three or four or five days a week at different times and adjust quite well when the schedule is not altered too often and their parents otherwise provide support and consistency in their lives. A chaotic, completely arbitrary (from the child's point of view) schedule would, of course, not be ideal for a young child, but a child who is raised with a varied schedule that takes his needs into account (such as when he is hungry and tired) can benefit.

One area that is sometimes problematic for single parents is home management. If you have always been a single parent, you may not be as bothered; but if you are new to single parenthood, having previously relied on someone else to be there, now you need to organize certain activities and prepare for certain possibilities, particularly with a young child. In regard to the usual household activities—laundry, washing, folding, putting away; shopping; cooking; cleaning; and child care—it is important to decide which things you have to do yourself, which the children can manage, and which you have to hire someone to do. In regard to possible emergencies, one single parent called it preparing for the "law of maximum inconvenience." That means that it is especially important, particularly at night, to have on hand the phone numbers for a pediatrician, dentist, poison-control center, plumber, electrician, and all-night drugstore, as well as that of a babysitter who might be available on short notice.

Visitation and other aspects of your child's relationship with your former spouse are likely to be of concern to you as a single parent. Even though you may be very angry with your former spouse, it is not fair to your child to separate him from his other parent, especially as a form of punishment. A child is not a piece of property that may be assigned to one or the other parent exclusively. You might want to consider shared custody or some other arrangement whereby both parents share responsibility for the child's welfare. Of course, that is not always possible, but if you don't try to sabotage yur former spouse's visits with your child, it will ultimately be in everyone's best interest. Avoid reprimanding your former spouse or arguing about finances when he or she comes to visit. You may need to deny visitation because of lack of financial support or because of a failure to come as scheduled, but again, try to be as flexible as possible to keep the lines of communication open between your child and his other parent. With young children especially, visitation is most likely to keep emotional and financial support coming from the absent parent.

Young children can be very manipulative. Your child may make you feel guilty about not being as "nice" as the absent parent. Single parents have no monopoly on guilt, but they sometimes fall prey to excessive guilt related to their single-parent status. You may feel guilty about not having tried hard enough to keep the family intact. Your child may blame the divorce on you because, as the remaining parent, it appears that you "kicked the other parent out" for being bad. In fact, this may make your child particularly sensitive in this area. He may feel, "If I am bad, will I get kicked out, too?" A male child might feel that you have something against males (which at that time might be so). All of this is very guilt-arousing, which in turn reduces your confidence and makes you vulnerable. Your parents, whether they are helpful to you as a single parent or not, may still appear to blame you for not "sticking it out." You might also feel guilty about dating. You may be more reluctant to leave your child with a babysitter than you would otherwise be, and perhaps your child, sensing this, may put up more than the usual resistance to your leaving. If you find a competent sitter, it is important that you go out, for the child's sake as well as your own. As we pointed out, you may feel guilty about rebuilding your own life. As we've said, this is generally helpful if you don't do it to the exclusion of a concern for the child's emotional as well as physical needs. Your young child will need you during a transitional period especially, but not exclusively. It is important for his own security to discover that other people can take care of him when you are not around and that you will return as you've promised. One of the great dangers in single parenthood is that your child may become too dependent on you.

Young children are usually not able to voice all of their concerns (this is especially true of infants, of course), but frequently children whose parents have separated or divorced do share some common concerns. You may not detect all of these in your child, but it is nonetheless helpful to be aware of them. One concern of your child in this situation is "What's wrong with me?" Very often, when couples separate or children are separated from their parents through divorce or death, the children feel that somehow they have done something wrong which has caused this to happen. Sometimes they actively search in their minds for the causes. Very often this whole question is not articulated, but it does have a very significant effect on the child's picture of himself.

Another common result of the separation process for children is feeling "I am being deprived"; that is, "I don't have what other children have." While this is not statistically the case, since more than half the young children today are raised in single-parent households, the feeling of loss is apt to be there, even if the child is too young to verbalize it. This feeling can lead to additional feelings of insecurity related to the "What's wrong with me?" question or a feeling of anger or rage at the dirty blow life has dealt. This is a familiar feeling because it occurs for the adults in the process, too. Sometimes it is hard to help a child when you are feeling this way yourself, but it is important not to feed into this feeling. You will probably find that if you can help your child to overcome some of the feelings of being deprived, you will feel better, too. The best approach here is to focus on what you have. You may be able to spend more constructive time together than when you were married. The household may be freer of tension and arguing. You may both have more time to do what you want to do. In some cases your ex-spouse may be a better parent to your child now that you are not together. In any case, if feelings of deprivation are getting your child or you down, take an inventory of what you have. You will probably be pleasantly surprised. Also, you may discover that whatever you need, you may be able to do for yourself. Becoming independent is a good feeling.

If you are a single parent, let us remind you again that all of the ideas that we have discussed throughout this book apply to you and your child. Communication is especially important, for example, since your child might ultimately have lots of questions about your divorce or the loss of his parent through death. If you listen carefully and try not to be too defensive or too protective, you will probably find that you can answer his questions honestly at a level he can understand. If you are alone, you are likely to find the tips on selecting babysitters and preschools very helpful, as well as the advice on creative activities for children. Managing as a single parent can help you to learn about your personal strengths and competencies. Your child may discover that you are not always "up" but that you are someone who can be counted on, and that's what matters most.

ADDITIONAL READING

HOPE, KAROL, and YOUNG, NANCY, eds., *Momma: The Sourcebook for Single Mothers*. New York: New American Library, 1976.

MCFADDEN, MICHAEL, *Bachelor Fatherhood: How to Raise and Enjoy Your Children as a Single Parent*. New York: Walker, 1974.

WATTS, VIRGINIA, *Single Parents*. Old Tappan, N.J.: Fleming H. Revell Co., 1976.

chapter thirteen
WORKING PARENTS

While there are increasing numbers of parents working today, many parents still have a conflict about it. Some say, "I have to work. What can I do to work and raise my family properly?" Others say, "I want to work and have a child. Can it be done? How?"

There is still a great deal of societal pressure against both parents', particularly mothers', working. Much of society feels that a mother's place is in the home, and this translates into guilt for the working mother and a lack of support and understanding for the adjustments she must make. One argument that has been voiced against a mother's working is that working parents do not spend enough time with their children. Yet when parents are home all the time, they do not necessarily interact with their children all the time, either. Sometimes they clean, cook, do laundry, watch TV, talk on the telephone, read, have visitors for coffee, or engage in extensive volunteer and social activities. As trite as it may sound, it is the quality of the time spent with the children that counts, not the quantity. Research has shown that mothers who are unhappy at home are not the most effective parents. Satisfied working parents probably spend more quality time with their children than parents who are at home against their will.

If you need to work for economic reasons but would prefer to be at home with your child, you may be able to get along on somewhat less income or to do some work at home such as typing or even caring for another child to help financially. On the other hand, if you would prefer to continue your career outside of the home or would simply like to work or to continue your education, you can delegate the responsibility for the care of your child to someone else while you are working without sacrificing the welfare of your child.

HOW DO MOTHERS AND CHILDREN FARE WHEN MOTHERS WORK?

A study of 280 families in Syracuse indicated that mothers who worked part-time experienced the most stress. Those who did not work at all ranked second, while full-time working mothers had the least stress.

In part-time work, women generally have to balance work and home duties. Unless there has been a clear clarification of roles and responsibilities, fathers often slack off more on household and children when wives are around. When women work full-time, however, their husbands seem to be more conscientious about participating in household activities.

In addition, working mothers seem to look at their child's development more objectively. Their children are less apt to be extensions of themselves, and they can thus be more accepting of their child's shortcomings. Children of working parents tend to exhibit more initiative, consideration, ability to help others, and self-sufficiency than most children of nonworking parents. This seems like a very favorable comparison. In addition, and very important in these times, daughters of working women particularly seem to have a greater sense of independence and a higher opinion of their sex and their abilities.

WAYS TO MANAGE WORKING AND CHILD RAISING

In some families, parents always worked; as the children grew up, they just grew into that lifestyle. In others, a parent may be returning to work or going back to school after several years of being at home. But even when there are varying schedules or when parents work different shifts, they still manage to share child rearing and household activities.

Sometimes we are given a distorted picture of what the working parent should be like, particularly the working woman. A newspaper article recently portrayed a woman, in a family with nine children, who holds a job, does the laundry, goes to courses, and continues to raise the nine children effectively. That is commendable, perhaps, but it is hardly realistic. We agree that you can work and raise children at the same time, but it is almost impossible to be an effective full-time mother, wife, housekeeper, and worker outside of the home all at the same time. There are ways to organize the activities in the house so that other family members shoulder a major share of the effort. Part of that decision rests with how you define growing with your children and how you look at developing personhood and parenthood together for you and your child.

Housework

We've raised some of these issues earlier in the chapter on non-sexist child rearing. Traditionally we expected that mothers could change diapers, cook meals, keep house, and administer to the emotional needs of the family. No one ever expects that a mother can't, even if she hasn't been trained. What about fathers? We've noted that they should be equally capable and expected to share in the parenting and housekeeping activities.

Children are also helpful in carrying out some home-management activities. At the age when they are developing autonomy and initiative, they like to contribute to household activities and feel useful and competent in the family. As we said earlier, children learn by their own activities with concrete materials, such as sorting the laundry, unpacking groceries, and setting the table. These are activities that they like and that contribute to the development of their independence and competence, in addition to helping you.

Cooking and Shopping

In addition to dividing household responsibilities, many working parents have found it helpful to organize their time more efficiently by cooking several meals in advance on the weekend to be served during the week when they are working. Shopping time can be reduced by having a list of groceries that need to be bought on the refrigerator or a bulletin board in the kitchen and getting everyone to note when an item has run out. Combining that with a once-a-week major shopping trip, rather than many little trips, will be more efficient and will save time and energy.

Outside Help

There is one another option that working families sometimes use. That is to secure outside help. As we noted in the chapter on single parents, you have to decide what you have to do, what the children can do, and what you must hire someone to do. It may be better for your particular child and family to spend some of your earnings on obtaining some quality child care and, if possible, some outside help with housecleaning. Sometimes if you try to do everything yourself as the mother or even if both parents participate, this leaves very little time and energy to enjoy your child and each other.

SPECIAL ISSUES
WHEN PARENTS WORK

Some parents both work and go to school in order to improve their education and their career opportunities. This makes their time even more limited. Here again, dividing jobs and having children work with you washing dishes, folding laundry, and cooking becomes time shared together as well as tasks completed.

If your child is at a child care center for many hours, it is particularly important to visit the center for a short time, both morning and evening, if possible. Reserving even a very few minutes to read, talk, or have a special time together at home in the evenings is also very important in these instances. On the weekends, plan to set aside some time for baking cookies or even a whole day for some special excursion or just being together with your child. You can increase the time you have together by taking your child along on errands, but that's not the same as reserving some time that is especially oriented toward her.

Sometimes parents who work worry because they may be missing some of the precious or formative experiences of their children. Setting aside time to do some of the activities we mentioned earlier will provide occasions where you can share some of those memorable moments.

SUMMARY

Certainly a mother's working requires adjustments in the family, but enlisting the father as coparent and the children in participation in household activities are positive adjustments, not negative actions. And if they are accomplished with children early enough, it becomes part of a team effort and a way of life, a part of the growing experience of parents and children.

ADDITIONAL READING

OLDS, SALLY W., "When Mommy Goes to Work," *Family Health/ Today's Health,* February 1977.

U.S. DEPARTMENT OF LABOR, Women's Bureau, *Working Mothers and Their Children,* 1977.

"Working Mother," *McCall's,* October 1978.

chapter fourteen
FINDING AND CHOOSING CHILD CARE

The demand for child care services is increasing all the time. There are women working, more single parent families, more two-earner families, more parents seeking further career and educational opportunities, and more families living away from their relatives. In addition, more parents are aware of research findings that report the benefits of early childhood programs for young children.

Child care as we use the term in this chapter includes families' taking care of children, babysitters, family day care homes, play groups, and child care programs. The range of choices for child care varies from community to community, both in nature and quantity. Some communities offer an array of choices in types of programs and caregivers. In other places there are not enough child care services to go around.

Your own first child care requirement may simply be to choose a babysitter for an evening or an afternoon. On the other hand, it may be that you must locate an all-day program in order to return to work or a part-day program, an educational or social experience for your child.

How do you find substitute child care services? Then, once you find them, how do you choose what kind of child care is best for your needs? How do you pick a particular caregiver or

154

program? There have been several pocket-size booklets prepared about choosing child care. We'll reference them at the end of the chapter. We felt it important at least to address the issue of choosing child care here by describing the kinds of child care available in many communities and providing some principles and practices upon which to base your choices.

How do you find out what kind of child care services are available in your town? Some communities are fortunate enough to have a child care information and referral center. In most communities, however, you must rely on word-of-mouth from parent to parent, signs in supermarkets and churches, the yellow pages, or newspaper advertisements.

What kind of child care is likely to be available?

CHILD CARE OPTIONS

Child Care in Your Own Home

The usual way to provide child care in your own home is to hire a sitter or relative who comes and takes care of your child while you are away. The babysitter may just watch a sleeping child, if you are only out for the evening, or the sitter may be responsible for the day-to-day care of your child while you are out working or going to school.

There are several advantages to arranging child care in your own home. The setting is familiar to your child. If you are working, your child does not have to be dressed before you go to work. After-school care, babysitting at night, and children who are sick are less of a problem when someone takes care of your child in your own home.

Substitute child care at home for more than an occasional babysitting need is often difficult to find and expensive when found. You may put an ad in a local newspaper or inquire at a local college. Your community may have a referral service or a community bulletin board. In some communities retired persons, teachers, and students will provide this kind of service for you in exchange for room and board. In other communities there may be a homemaker service or an agency where women are trained in child care and homemaking.

In addition to the expense and the scarcity of this kind of child care service, there are a few other limitations. One is that no one supervises the sitter while that person is actually taking care of your child; there is no one to see that what you have asked is really being done. More often than not, a child, particularly an infant, will not be able to tell you how things went. For that reason, references, prior experience, and an extensive interview with the person are very important before you make your selection. Another limitation is that sometimes the babysitter gets sick or is otherwise unavailable. In some cases an employer will allow parents to take sick days to care for their children. Other times parents have been able to arrange a back-up system with relatives or friends. But if those options aren't available, there can be a real problem. Some people use a relative as a sitter. That can be a problem too. Parents have told us that relatives are often not reliable about following instructions. Several mothers interviewed by the authors took child-care responsibilities for their children away from a sister and a mother because they were permitting the children to watch too much television and not providing them with enough stimulating activities.

Play Groups

Play groups are informal cooperative groups organized by parents comprised of a few children who are about the same age, usually within a four-month age difference from each other. They generally meet twice a week for about two hours at a time. The sessions are usually held at different houses on a rotating basis. Optimally all the locations are within walking distance from each other. On occasion there are play groups with as many as twenty children. Those with large enrollments usually hire a teacher.

The play group provides a good first social and play experience for children. It also provides parents of young children with a chance to get to know one another. But there are some limitations to play groups, too. In most cases, if you have more than one child, only one is eligible for the play group. Another difficulty is that parents, although well-intentioned, don't always know what children should do. Most important, the sessions are brief and only allow for a limited time away from your child. A parent can really only use play groups during errands or appointments but not for employment or school unless they are combined with another child care service.

Family Day Care

Family day care usually refers to child care services in another person's home. Sometimes there are up to six children with one adult, other times up to twelve children with two adults. If the family day care program is run by an agency, the mothers are often trained and supervised. Family day care programs that are licensed have regulations governing safety and health, though very few of them have regulations covering the program offered to the children.

A family day care home can be like a home away from home. Daily life goes on, and the children can be part of the activities of running a house. A family day care provider can do many of the activities discussed in our chapters on practical and creative activities in the home and short trips in the community. There are likely to be mixed age groups in family day care homes, making them good settings for learning. Infants and toddlers are apt to have more individual attention in a well-run family day care home. Often the home can take care of more than one child in a family and, in some, even a mildly ill child is accepted.

As positive as those characteristics are, there are also limitations to family day care homes. Some homes may not be licensed. Others may have too little supervision, too much TV, and too few activities. Then, too, here as with a babysitter, what happens if the provider gets sick?

Child Care Centers

There have been child care programs of an educational or custodial nature since before the turn of the century. Originally day care centers focused primarily on the physical care of the child while mothers worked, while traditional nursery schools and laboratory schools focused more on education. That is not the case today. Both day care centers and nursery schools have different degrees of commitment to education and child care. That commitment is usually determined by the person in charge of the center.

The child care center may be a part-day program, a full-day program, a flexible-schedule program, or an after-school program. Some centers are open full-time all year round; others follow a school calendar.

CHOOSING APPROPRIATE CHILD CARE

There are some general questions to consider when choosing child care. What does it cost? What are your transportation needs? What hours and days do you require? Then there are the more person-centered considerations: How old is your child? Is your child an infant who may do best with one adult tending to the majority of her needs in her own home? Is your child a four-year-old who would have fun with a fourteen-year-old in a home babysitting situation? Is your child a shy child who is having a first experience with child care and might do well in a small family day care setting? Or do you have an outgoing child who may thrive in a large center with a variety of children's activities and adults with whom to interact?

Are you a single parent who would want a center-based child care service that provides a variety of support systems for parents, including counseling and auxiliary services such as medical, dental, hearing, and vision testing for children as well as meals?

Suppose you've decided on family day care or center-based child care to meet your needs. Then how do you choose one particular child care service? We feel that it is very important to visit the program. Actually, it is helpful if you can visit several programs before making a decision even if you like the very first one you visit. You should try to stay for an extended period of time or make several short visits in order to see how the morning is spent, how transitions are made from one activity to another, and how the afternoon is planned. First visits are best made without your children, who may tire quickly or may hang on you or misbehave. While you are observing, you might ask yourself, How will my child fare in this setting? If your child is particularly fond of or in need of large areas for physical activity, does the center have space to fill her needs? Does she expend a lot of energy in bicycling, running, jumping? Do you want your child to be inventive? If so, are there opportunities to plan projects, choose interests, use materials in innovative ways?

Do you feel at home there? What do they expect of you as a parent? These questions apply equally well to center-based care, family day care, or a play group. Talk to the director, then talk to the teachers and especially other parents, who may be more candid than the director, about the strengths and weaknesses of the program.

As parents visiting a center, we would focus on the people first and the program second. Then we would examine the health and safety aspects of the program, the equipment, the food, and the auxiliary services. All aspects of the child care services are important, but if the personnel or program are inadequate, we would not consider the rest if there is a choice available. If there is no choice, then as a parent it would be time to campaign for different conditions and more qualified day care.

You might make a variety of observations about the people. Are the caregivers warm and responsive? Are they consistent in their actions toward the children? Do they bend down to the children's eye level to talk to them? Do they seem to enjoy working with the children? Are they affectionate in their physical relationship, greeting the children on arrival, acknowledging their departure, allowing time for lap sitting and hugging? Do the caregivers practice consistent and positive discipline rather than negative or abusive punishment? What do they do if a child is restless? Do they try to help the children solve their own problems and develop self-control? Are there enough adults, but not too many? Do the boys and girls seem to be treated equally?

Are their racial, socioeconomic, and cultural backgrounds respected?

Do the adults support children's play by providing appropriate materials? Are the children given a choice of materials and allowed to do their own designs and placements, or is most of the work done by the teacher with just a slight directed touch by each child? Do the caregivers participate in the children's activities instead of standing and talking by themselves or working alone, ignoring the children?

During your visit, take a look at the children themselves. Do they seem to be having fun? Are they involved, or are they wandering aimlessly? How do they treat each other? Do they respect each other? Do they help each other? Do they enjoy working together? How do the adults relate to one another? What kind of atmosphere do they create? Did the staff interview you before inviting you to enroll your child? Did they encourage you to observe? Did they greet you and talk to you about your child? Do parents, children, and teachers talk to each other when children arrive or are ready to leave?

In regard to the program, do the director and teachers have written plans and a schedule for what the children will do? Even if you value spontaneity, that doesn't prohibit planning. Are there a variety of activities for children of different age and development levels, with choices available to the children at each level? Is there an outdoor playground? Rest periods? Cleanup? Is the change from one activity to another accomplished without too much waiting time for the children or whining by the children?

Is the room light and clean, with enough space for both active and quiet play as well as privacy? Does the center have child-sized furniture? Is there a variety of equipment and toys, including transporation toys (trucks, a gas station, trains), construction toys, blocks, Tinkertoys, a drama corner with dress-up materials and homemaking props? Is there an area for art activities, a science corner with materials to explore, a music area with a record player and instruments, a special place for books? Are the materials accessible to the children in these areas?

Is the yard fenced in? Is the bathroom clean? Is there a first-aid kit? Is there a change of clothes for every child? Are health forms required?

Is the kitchen clean? Have the menus been posted? Are the meals and snacks nutritional? Do the portions look adequate? Does the center serve a midmorning and afternoon snack? Do the children seem to like the food? Do the children help prepare the food? Do the teachers join the children and talk during snacks or lunch?

If you are visiting a family day care home, you would look for the same kind of adult-child interaction as we mentioned for observing child care centers. You also want to know what the family day care mother believes about raising children. Is what she believes in accordance with your position on child care and child rearing? If there are differences, are they acceptable to you? Children can be in different settings where there are different expectations for behavior, but all of the people with whom you entrust the care of your child should respect the values and goals most important to you.

At a child care center, you usually see all the staff. In a family day care home, it is important to find out who else besides the family day care provider will take care of the children. As in the center, you will want to watch the provider play with the children. You will also want to know what kind of program she or he plans. You will want to see all the places that the children will be able to use. You should discuss development, health and safety practices, and discipline with your family day care provider. A family day care mother should also know where you can be reached and have her own plans for emergencies and special needs.

In the case of at-home care, it is important to have a sitter come to your house a few times to see how she or he plays with your child before deciding whom to entrust with the care of your child in your home without you.

Discuss the sitter's ideas about child care. How does she or he feel about discipline? About children and TV? The earlier questions about caregivers' interactions with children apply equally well here.

If you have decided to hire someone, let the person come and watch you spend time with your child. This way she or he can observe how you interact with your child. Then have the sitter spend some time with the child alone while you are in another part of the house. A person who is going to care for your child needs to be informed about development and health and safety practices. That person should know how to encourage language and develop a child's curiosity. You should discuss discipline, rituals, specific play, and books to read, even with a sitter who is only going to provide child care for a short time. You and the sitter should talk about your child and your child's habits as fully as possible.

A sitter caring for your child in your home should know how to locate you immediately. Telephone numbers of the doctor, hospital, and neighbors should be posted. Special instructions and schedules for your children should be discussed and written out.

Precautions When Choosing Child Care

We would question a program if the person in charge won't let you observe. We would also question a program where the adults do not respond to the children or use angry, rough voices or manners. Other alarm signals include a dirty setting, an unsafe setting, and children who look and seem unhappy.

INTRODUCING YOUR CHILD TO A CENTER

Once you have contracted for child care, it is then necessary to prepare yourself and your child for the experience. How you do that depends on whether the person is coming to your home or you are going to bring your child to a center.

If you have decided on a child care program after having visited and observed it yourself, it is very helpful for you to visit it with your child a few times. First arrange to stay as long as your child does. Give your child a chance to get to know the setting or the person they are being left with. This gives you and the teacher a chance to observe your child in that setting, of course, but it is also important for your child to get comfortable before you leave her, especially if this is her first group care experience. When you go to a new place or a party, you may look around first and assess the situation. You don't necessarily get right into the crowd. Neither do children. Your child may cling to you; that's to be expected. Some children get to know a place by standing next to their parent and looking. Others plunge in but make sure their parents are there by occasionally returning. Others want their parent to come around with them. Sometimes children leave their coats on so as to be able to leave or to show they are not ready to commit themselves. Your child may not necessarily talk to anyone or even play with anything at first. Or she may push and pull. In the latter case, she will need to be restrained gently and guided, but it may be her way of trying the place out. Whatever the child does, it is her way of becoming familiar with the setting, and it is all right as long as it does not interfere with a program or the rights of other children.

If you've chosen wisely and are comfortable with your choice, separation will occur smoothly. Stay a few minutes, tell your child you are leaving, and leave. More often it's the parents who have a problem leaving. Lingering shows your anxiety and generally causes a reaction in a child. If you can arrange to be contacted and available in case of a problem during the first days, that is helpful. In ten years of nursery school experience with close to a thousand children, only two or three times have parents had to be called back, and it was generally because the parents were anxious and transmitted this to their child before they separated. We have also discovered that often children who do not seemed pleased about being left get very involved once their parent leaves. It may take your child a few days to get really relaxed and involved. Don't panic. The wait and possible discomfort are worthwhile in the long run. The independent experience that your child has in a child care center is a major step in the development of her own identity and a sense of her own competence apart from you. Sometimes that's difficult for parents to handle, but it's another very important example of growing together.

ADDITIONAL READING

AUERBACH, STEVANNE, AND FREEDMAN, LINDA, *Choosing Child Care: A Guide for Parents*. Parent and Child Care Resources, San Francisco, 1976.

CENTER FOR SYSTEMS AND PROGRAM DEVELOPMENT, INC., *A Parent's Guide to Day Care*. DHHS Publication No. (OHDS) 80–30254, March 1980. This manual is available from Day Care Division, Administration for Children, Youth and Family, HEW, P.O. Box 1182, Washington, D.C. 20013.

CHILDREN'S DEFENSE FUND, *A Child Advocate's Guide to Capitol Hill*. Washington, 1980.

COBB, FAYE, *A Parent's Guide to Better Babysitting*. New York: Pocket Books, 1963.

COMPREHENSIVE COMMUNITY CHILD CARE, *Selecting Quality Child Care for Parents of Young Children*. Cincinnati, 1979.

GOLD, JANE R., and BERGSTRUM, JOAN M., *Checking Out Child Care*. Day Care and Child Development Council of America, 1975.

SHEA, JANET, and SMITH, PAUL V., *Where Do You Look? Whom Do You Ask? How Do You Know? Information for Child Advocates*. Washington: Children's Defense Fund, 1980.

chapter fifteen
THE PARENT AS ADVOCATE

In the early days families were considered self-sufficient. They were the institutions that provided care for all members of the family including the disabled and the elderly. But that role of the family has changed, and with that the parents' roles and functions. There are social and economic forces that affect parents and children in spite of what they personally do or feel. We now share our child rearing with many other institutions—schools, churches, federal government, and television—and it has become necessary to become an advocate for our own children in particular and children in general in a variety of areas.

Parents sometimes throw up their hands and declare that "it is impossible." Children are influenced by such a wide range of experiences that seem to be beyond their ability to control. Sometimes a child with special needs can't get services. There may be only inadequate child care available. Children may be abused or ignored in the schools or the child care centers. Parents face a variety of frustrations with many of these institutions.

Yet there are areas that are within a parent's sphere of influence, some which you may not have realized. Parenthood requires that you make many active choices on behalf of your child, and as an advocate and decision maker you can help maximize your child's positive experiences.

Even before birth, as a child's advocate, a mother's choice of diet and exercise can help to influence her child's later development. As a prospective parent, you have a right to help decide how your child will be born. If you want a natural child-birth, for example, or want both parents involved in the delivery, you need not accept an obstetrician's dismissal of the idea. You can choose to seek additional professional advice. This applies later to the decision about breast-feeding as well. Obstetricians may have personal preferences which may contrast with parents' wishes. These preferences are not necessarily correct for you and your situation.

Later, at home, you make decisions about the use of a nurse or other caretaker when the child first comes home from the hospital. There may be a lot of people, including your own parents and so-called "experts," giving advice on how to handle things, but ultimately the decision is and should be yours as a parent.

There is no question that a child will change your life style. Where does advocacy fit in here? Your selection of substitute care, your option to stay home with the baby or to work, your decision to enroll the child in a play group or preschool—all are active choices that require consideration of the child's needs.

If there are older children, a place for the new baby needs to be created. This is another form of advocacy. It is wise to prepare older children for the birth of a new child, representing the new child who cannot speak for himself, while exercising caution to prevent making too much of the new arrival. It is important to help the other children understand why the baby takes their things and needs you so much. These things are not always easy for the older ones to accept, though active work on a parent's part sometimes helps. It is wise to admit that the new baby isn't always wonderful and is in fact frequently a great deal of trouble for you as well as the older children.

Another sphere of home advocacy may be your decisions concerning sleeping and eating. You might decide very early not to feed your baby junk food in the form of some prepared foods.

You might also help your baby regulate his sleep pattern in a way that is acceptable to the baby, you, and your family.

Outside the family, you might have to advocate in terms of visits or type of handling by relatives. Although you can't expect grandparents to do things precisely as you do, you do have the right to prevent what you might consider mishandling by them or other adults. This is true with babysitters and teachers, too. It is important to share your point of view about child rearing before engaging such helpmates if there are any basic disagreements. In addition, it is important to continue to discuss a child's treatment by others who are caring for him.

Still in the area of home decisions, parents have complex choices in regard to child rearing. Parents need to choose a community in which to live, a school, a doctor, perhaps even a special program to fit the child's needs.

As you begin to move out from home and interact with other agencies, there are other advocacy roles available to you. Some mothers start by joining a support group themselves. Mothers' centers have been developing in areas where parents have found that community services do not meet their needs. Organizing themselves as groups, they have been planning their own programs and courses. These mothers' centers range from places to drop a child off and shop a little or talk with other mothers to more formal organizations that have paid staff and promote legislative changes and services for parents. The mothers in one center campaigned for sibling visitation rights in hospital maternity wards. In another center, they compiled a survey of maternity and pediatric options in their area.

Other parents find advocacy necessary in relation to child care centers. Child care centers can act as a second or extended family if the center has a responsible staff. On the other hand, an unresponsive center can cause pressures on parents to multiply. In those cases, it becomes essential to advocate for good communication and services. One parent may want to press for parent conferences from five to seven for working parents. Another parent may want to advocate for alternative child care arrangements for snow days, vacations, and holidays. Some parents may want to pilot a program for sick children. Some parents may want more extensive dialogue about what their children are doing. Others want to sensitize caregivers to parents' problems, for example, why some parents feel pressed to bring children who are a little sick or unkempt in the morning.

Advocacy for children extends past early childhood programs. Some parents in the public schools have established day care centers where mothers take turns taking care of the children, who play while the other mothers volunteer in public schools. Some mothers petition for traffic lights or send letters to support teenage jobs or a candidate who favors child care services. Those are all forms of advocacy. Still others have arranged for a prenatal program in a hospital which includes sessions on parenting. Even PTAs have moved from just sponsoring schoolwide programs to a more active role for parents, becoming involved in such issues as TV violence, handicapped children, school finance. Others may begin to advocate for parenting courses in junior and senior high school and hospitals. Maybe you are concerned about junk food and promoting good nutrition for children, or maybe you want to make an impact on the toy industry, where there seems to be a woeful lack of interest in children, toy makers being only interested in their profits. You may be a working parent who wants to join others to advocate for maternity leaves, days to take care of sick children, flextime, day care at your work site, or after-school programs until five and school conferences in early morning or evening. As you can see, there are lots of areas that affect children that would benefit from parent advocacy.

Some communities, in addition to mothers' centers, day care center groups, and PTAs, have local advocacy services. Some have been formed by parents who have worked hard through their own PTA or for their own children and have joined efforts to help others. In one case, two parents, both of whom had children with special needs, decided to use their expertise in advocating for their children and their educational background to help other parents by forming an advocacy service. In other cases, parents of gifted children have begun their own school because they were displeased with the public school services for their children with special needs. Parents of children with developmental disabilities have also needed to organize to get increased programs and research. This has been very effective and has raised the consciousness of professionals as well as legislators.

There are national advocacy agencies, too. Action for Children's Television (ACT) is a national advocacy organization that began as an informal meeting of parents, teachers, and television professionals who were all concerned about the excessive violence on TV for children. They founded ACT in 1976 as a consumer organization to improve broadcasting practices that related to children. The organization was concerned about the values, problem situations, crime, and aspects of sexuality that children are exposed to on TV. It was also concerned with advertising and wanted to ban it, suggesting that children are not a match for sophisticated advertising, especially since they don't really understand the difference between the program and advertising.

The Children's Defense Fund is another national advocacy organization that was founded to try to make an impact on specific issues in Congress. Their areas of concern are education health care, child care and development, child welfare, and juvenile justice. They have a legislative agenda and try to make sure children's needs are not shortchanged.

Each of these national organizations has membership dues and is supported by foundations and grants. Each one puts out publications on your role as an advocate and would benefit from your active involvement.

Why would you advocate? We think it's important for both the children and yourself. Young children cannot speak out for themselves, and they, both our own and other people's children, need someone to speak out for them. They are our future and will be in charge of our society tomorrow. It is in our interest that they grow up healthy, and we should not leave that to chance alone. In addition, advocacy works. Parent power has pioneered school reforms, opened new programs for gifted and handicapped children, and raised public consciousness to their needs. Parent power has made an impact on clinical medicine, research, government agencies, and the needs of special children.

As we begin to speak out, we gain personal power. We begin to address some of the social and economic problems that face our society; by taking a problem of manageable size, getting facts, and joining others, we can make a positive difference. Advocacy provides numerous satisfactions to those who participate as well as those who directly benefit from it.

As you help your child grow, you grow too, in stature and in personhood, and in turn so does society.

FOR MORE INFORMATION

ACT (ACTION FOR CHILDREN'S TELEVISION), 46 Austin Street, Newtonville, Massachusetts 02160
CHILDREN'S DEFENSE FUND, 1520 New Hampshire Avenue N.W., Washington, D.C. 20036

REFLECTIONS

Having read all the chapters, you're probably thinking "and now what?" I still have to get through those "terrible-two's days," the whining, the fights. And I'm still not sure if I'm doing it right. Is this typical? Does this happen to anyone else? Some people have been known to resort to looking up descriptions in Gesell's *Infant and Child in the Culture of Today* to see if their children sound similar to what Gesell described as normal. A pediatrician friend used to say "and this, too, shall pass," but it still has to be dealt with.

Now that you have read about development, and hopefully have taken time to think about your own values and your own style, it's useful to reflect on some of the time you spend with your child. What happened? Why did you do what you did? Why did your child do what she did? Did you expect too much? Or were you out of sorts? Or is it a new developmental stage, and some of what was all right before now needs to be modified? Distancing yourself by reflecting is often enough to allow you to extend your patience and understand what's happening on the most frustrating days and savor the fun and delight of the most satisfying times. We hope that in time you will be able to be relaxed and appreciate your child's language, her involvement in your activities, her perception of the world and engage in child rearing in a more enthusiastic way.

171

INDEX